TOP 10
BUENOS AIRES

DECLAN MCGARVEY
JONATHAN SCHULTZ

EYEWITNESS TRAVEL

Contents

Left **Tango show** Center **Painting at Kelly's shop** Right **Cementerio de la Recoleta**

LONDON, NEW YORK,
MELBOURNE, MUNICH AND DELHI
www.dk.com

Design, Editorial, and Picture Research, by
Quadrum Solutions, Krishnamai, 33B,
Sir Pochkanwala Road, Worli, Mumbai, India

Printed and bound in China by
Leo Paper Products Ltd

First American Edition, 2009
13 14 15 16 10 9 8 7 6 5 4 3 2 1

Published in the United States by
DK Publishing, 375 Hudson Street,
New York, New York 10014

Reprinted with revisions 2011, 2013

**Copyright 2009, 2013 © Dorling Kindersley
Limited, London, A Penguin Company**

Published in the UK by Dorling Kindersley Limited.

A catalog record for this book is available
from the Library of Congress.

ISSN: 1479-344X

ISBN: 978-0-7566-9679-5

Within each Top 10 list in this book, no hierarchy of
quality or popularity is implied. All 10 are, in the
editor's opinion, of roughly equal merit.

Floors are referred to throughout in accordance
with American usage; ie the "first floor" is the floor
above ground level.

MIX
Paper from
responsible sources
FSC™ C018179

Contents

Buenos Aires' Top 10

Buenos Aires' Highlights 6

Plaza de Mayo 8

Cementerio de la
Recoleta 10

Teatro Colón 12

Avenida de Mayo 14

Museo Nacional de
Bellas Artes 16

San Telmo 18

Avenida 9 de Julio 20

MALBA 22

Colonia del Sacramento,
Uruguay 24

Tango 26

Moments in History 32

The information in this DK Eyewitness Top 10 Travel Guide is checked regularly.
Every effort has been made to ensure that this book is as up-to-date as possible at the time of
going to press. Some details, however, such as telephone numbers, opening hours, prices,
gallery hanging arrangements and travel information are liable to change. The publishers
cannot accept responsibility for any consequences arising from the use of this book, nor for
any material on third party websites, and cannot guarantee that any website address in this
book will be a suitable source of travel information. We value the views and suggestions of
our readers very highly. Please write to: Publisher, DK Eyewitness Travel Guides,
Dorling Kindersley, 80 Strand, London WC2R 0RL, UK, or email: travelguides@dk.com.

Cover: Front – **Dorling Kindersley:** Rough Guides/Greg Roden bl; **AWL Images:** Danita Delimont Stock main.
Spine – **DK Images:** Demetrio Carrasco b. Back – **DK Images:** Demetrio Carrasco tl, tc, tr. .

Left **Exhibits at MALBA** Center **Café Tortoni** Right **Interior of Galerías Pacífico**

Striking Buildings   34

Plazas and Green Spaces   36

Argentinian Artisan
Stores   38

Intimate Museums   40

Festivals   42

Tango Clubs and Milongas 44

Nightclubs   46

Gay Clubs and Hangouts   48

Culinary Highlights   52

Parrillas   54

Restaurants   56

Porteño Personalities   58

Activities for Children   60

Around Town

Barrio Norte, Recoleta
& Around   64

San Telmo & La Boca   72

Microcentro, Puerto
Madero & Retiro   80

Palermo   86

Beyond Buenos Aires   94

Streetsmart

Practical Information   102

Places to Stay   112

General Index   118

Phrase Book   126

Left **El Caminito, La Boca** Right **Congreso Nacional**

BUENOS AIRES' TOP 10

Buenos Aires'
Highlights
6–7

Plaza de Mayo
8–9

Cementerio de
la Recoleta
10–11

Teatro Colón
12–13

Avenida de Mayo
14–15

Museo Nacional
de Bellas Artes
16–17

San Telmo
18–19

Avenida 9 de Julio
20–21

Museo de Arte
Latinoamericano de
Buenos Aires
22–23

Colonia del
Sacramento, Uruguay
24–25

Tango
26–29

TOP10 Buenos Aires' Highlights

Argentina's romantic, reinvigorated soul, Buenos Aires is la Capital, where tango combos keep time in crowded milongas (dance halls), young men cry out deliriously at gargantuan soccer stadiums, and taxis swap lanes across some of the world's widest avenues. Porteños, as the residents of this sophisticated metropolis are called, move to a rhythm all of their own, while making time to dine, dress, and even rest, extraordinarily well. With spectacular museums, lovely open spaces, and rich architecture brimming with history, the city is warm as well as energetic.

Plaza de Mayo 1

This square has seen post-World Cup soccer victory dances as well as the deafening silence of the Mothers of the Plaza de Mayo's weekly marches *(see pp8–9)*.

Cementerio de la Recoleta 2

As monument and metaphor for a country's fortunes – both gained and lost – la Recoleta contrasts impeccable mausoleums with crumbling marble tombs *(see pp10–11)*.

Teatro Colón 3

Having celebrated its centennial under scaffolding, the grandest of all Latin American opera houses opened in 2010 after an exhaustive restoration. El Colón is arguably the most beloved building in all of Argentina *(see pp12–13)*.

Avenida de Mayo 4

Buenos Aires' prized avenue is a boon to architecture buffs – it contains the continent's best preserved Belle Époque, Art Nouveau, and Art Deco addresses. Old bookstores and cafés add to the charm *(see pp14–15)*.

Museo Nacional de Bellas Artes 5

The modest scale of Argentina's national fine art museum belies a wonderfully curated permanent collection, which ranges from imposing Rodin bronzes to oils depicting the mythical Argentinian Pampa. The museum holds great works by many international artists *(see pp16–17)*.

Preceding pages **El Caminito, La Boca**

6 San Telmo

Among the city's oldest *barrios*, cobblestoned San Telmo guards the lyrical spirit of the *bodegón* – the quintessentially porteño bar/café where a vermouth or croissant can be arranged any time. Lanes lined with 19th-century homes brim with performers on Sundays *(see pp18–19)*.

7 Avenida 9 de Julio

The grandest of Latin American avenues is flanked by dozens of cultural highlights, the biggest of which is Teatro Colón. Take care when crossing its 12-lane width, which takes a few traffic-light cycles to accomplish *(see pp20–21)*.

8 Museo de Arte Latinoamericano de Buenos Aires (MALBA)

MALBA has quickly asserted itself since its 2001 opening. Its collection of Latin American artwork, which includes Diego Rivera and Xul Solar, has been supplemented with film screenings and a unique museum gift shop *(see pp22–23)*.

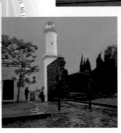

9 Colonia del Sacramento, Uruguay

Founded by Portuguese traders, Colonia is a picturesque town. Its colorful colonial streets, Portuguese architecture, and relaxed pace, make it a popular weekend spot *(see pp24–25)*.

10 Tango

Jaunty and humorous or dirge-like and mournful, tango – the capital's dance, musical, and poetic art form – is still in full swoon, 120 years after its creation. With classes and performances galore, it is integral to the city's culture and continues to captivate the people of Buenos Aires and the rest of the world *(see pp26–29)*.

Plaza de Mayo

Like spokes on a wheel, some of Buenos Aires' most important avenues radiate outward from Plaza de Mayo. Nearly every era of the city's history is reflected in the plaza's surroundings. The 18th-century government's diminutive seat of power, El Cabildo, is divested of any official duty, yet it still manages to exude an imposing aura opposite the much larger current executive governmental offices, the Casa Rosada. The landscaped space in between has been the scene of Argentina's fiercest internal struggles and greatest joys, from the naval attacks of 1955 to pulsating parties following World Cup soccer victories in 1978 and 1986. For all its formidable history, Plaza de Mayo can still offer a quiet bench to read the paper or sip a maté.

Plazoleta de San Francisco

🕐 If you are visiting between March and November, take a trip to the nearby Casa de la Cultura *(see p15)* for the free dance performances at 6pm.

🍴 Have cakes and coffee just two blocks away at Café La Puerto Rico *(Calle Alsina 420).*

• Map F2
• Casa Rosada: Calle Hipólito Yrigoyen 219; 4344-3802; www.museo.gov.ar
• El Cabildo: Calle Bolívar 65; 4342-6729; www.cultura.gov.ar
• La Catedral Metropolitana: Cnr Avda. Rivadavia & Calle San Martín; 4331-2845; www.catedralbuenos aires.org.ar
• Ministerio de Economía: Calle Hipólito Yrigoyen 250; 4349-5000; www.mecon.gov.ar

Top 10 Features

1. Casa Rosada
2. El Cabildo
3. La Catedral Metropolitana
4. Pirámide de Mayo
5. Las Madres de Plaza de Mayo
6. Banco de la Nación
7. Monument to General Belgrano
8. Protests
9. Ministerio de Economía
10. Plazoleta de San Francisco

1 Casa Rosada

The President holds meetings in the Casa Rosada *(above)*. Visitors can go back in time in the building's museum, containing artifacts from the city's original fortification.

2 El Cabildo

This viceroy government building, built in 1725, guards a collection of relics that hint at Argentina's pre-independence stature. Its rear patio hosts an artisans' market on Thursdays and Fridays.

3 La Catedral Metropolitana

This large Neo Classical cathedral *(below)* was consecrated in 1836. A look inside reveals a Rococo-style altar and the mausoleum of Argentina's liberator, General José de San Martín.

Pirámide de Mayo 4

The Pirámide *(right)* is dedicated to the revolutionaries of 1810, who orchestrated Argentina's independence. A nearby plaque commemorates Julio López, a key witness who went missing during a trial in 2006.

5 Las Madres de Plaza de Mayo

A plaza fixture since 1977, Las Madres are the defiant mothers of the young men and women who disappeared during the 1976–82 military dictatorship. Anyone is welcome to join in the weekly marches.

Banco de la Nación 6

The national bank contains an amusing scale model of the Plaza as it appeared during the bank's mid-20th-century construction, with fine details of pedestrians and cars. Also a showstopper is the building's superb central dome.

Monument to General Belgrano 7

Although not remembered as a great military tactician, General Manuel Belgrano is credited with designing Argentina's flag. He is thus depicted on horseback bearing the national colors *(above)*.

Protests 8

Befitting the political heart of the nation, lively protests *(left)* are staged nearly every day in and around the Plaza. Always peaceful, an exception was the riot of December 2001 *(see p33)*.

Ministerio de Economía 9

The Economy Ministry ushered in the Officialist architectural style, later championed by Perón *(see p35)*. Check the lobby for two brooding 1939 oil paintings by muralists Naguil and Quirós.

Plazoleta de San Francisco 10

This sculpture garden contains four marble figures that previously surrounded the Pirámide de Mayo. Individually, the statues represent Astronomy, Navigation, Geography, and Industry.

35 Years of Las Madres

Heralded with rock concerts, TV specials, and political interest, the Madres de la Plaza de Mayo marked 35 years in 2012. Despite a 1986 rift, the Madres' message has never been diluted or coopted. Today, their efforts are directed toward identifying young adults who, as infants, were taken away from their birth mothers, as well as bringing to justice ex-military officers from the dictatorship era.

For information on Argentina's history, **See pp32–3.**

⫷⫸10 Cementerio de la Recoleta

One of the world's great necropolises, the Recoleta Cemetery, located in the upscale, northern barrio of the same name, has been the burial place of choice for Argentina's elite since the mid-19th century. Presidents, military generals, artists, aristocracy, and, most famously, Eva Perón lie interred here in fabulous mausoleums of granite and bronze. Built tightly against each other, the tombs are visited via a labyrinth of streets and narrow passageways. The architectural styles are numerous and fascinating: grandiose Greek temples stand adjacent to diminutive Egyptian pyramids and Art Nouveau vaults are next to monumental cenotaphs. Added in 1881, an imposing Doric-columned entrance protects this extraordinary city of the dead.

Benediction Chapel

🅰 A number of tour operators arrange walking tours of the cemetery. You can also buy a map at the cemetery entrance.

🅰 Grab a coffee at La Biela *(see p70)*, a Parisian-style café and one-time haunt of the city's intelligentsia and the automobile racing fraternity.

• Map N4
• Junín 1790, btwn Guido and Vicente López
• 4803-1594
• Open 8am–5:45pm daily
• Free English-language guided tours: 9:30am, 11am, 2pm, 4pm Tue–Sun

Top 10 Features

1. Eva Duarte de Perón
2. The Leloir Family
3. Domingo Faustino Sarmiento
4. Benediction Chapel
5. José C. Paz
6. Pantheon of Outstanding Citizens
7. Dorrego-Ortíz Basualdo
8. Carlos Pellegrini
9. William Brown
10. Pantheon of the Fallen in the 1890 Revolution

1 Eva Duarte de Perón
Evita lies embalmed within this rather modest family vault *(below)*. Tribute plaques inscribed with fiery quotes such as, "I will return and be millions!" crowd its walls and flowers always adorn its entrance.

2 The Leloir Family
Built in the style of a Greek temple, this grandiose family mausoleum embodies the ambition and confidence of Argentina's 19th-century elite. Like many other tombs here, its sculptures were fashioned in the studios of Europe.

3 Domingo Faustino Sarmiento
Sarmiento, president of Argentina from 1868 to 1874, was a Freemason. His tomb, which he designed himself, bears Masonic symbols such as pyramids, compasses, and the "all-seeing eye."

4 Benediction Chapel
This 1882 chapel is unusual for the remarkable crucifix that stands over its small altar. Sculpted from marble by Italian artist Giulio Monteverde, the *Cristo Morto* shows Christ in death, on the cross.

José C. Paz

Resting place of the founder of *La Prensa* newspaper, this is the cemetery's most beautiful monument *(left)*. An allegory of the immortal soul, it depicts an angel leaving its body and hoisting the soul heavenward.

Pantheon of Outstanding Citizens

This historical corner of the cemetery contains the tombs of several Independence-era heroes. Alongside the tombs, cenotaphs commemorate other pivotal figures from the same period.

Dorrego-Ortíz Basualdo

This sepulcher *(above)* features both a crucifix and a menorah, symbolizing the conversion from Judaism to Catholicism of this family's ancestors on arrival in Argentina in the 16th century.

Carlos Pellegrini

As president in 1890, Pellegrini steered the country through a severe financial crisis. His magnificent tomb sees him issuing orders from atop his coffin. A female figure and child, symbolizing the republic and its future, stand at his feet.

William Brown

Brown's fame as founder of Argentina's navy is overshadowed in death by the tragic story of his daughter, whose ashes lie here too. She drowned herself after her fiancé's death.

Pantheon of the Fallen in the 1890 Revolution

This memorial *(right)* remembers the dead from the failed revolution. Sculptures depict workers brandishing rifles. Several leaders of the Radical Party are buried here.

Origins of the Cementerio de la Recoleta

This cemetery was built in 1822, on what was then the northern limit of the city. The land was confiscated by the Argentinian government from the Recoleta monks of the adjacent Pilar Church. The city's first public cemetery, it was used initially for the burial of freed slaves and the proletariat before it became the reserve of the rich from 1860s onward.

Souvenir books on the cemetery can be bought at the information stand near the entrance. Proceeds go to cemetery upkeep.

🔟 Teatro Colón

For its sheer size, near-perfect acoustics, and stately elegance, the Teatro Colón ranks among the world's top opera houses. Yet for porteños, the Neo-Classical structure represents far more. "Rich as an Argentine" was a phrase regularly heard on the streets of New York and Paris around the theater's 1908 completion, and to experience the Colón's grandeur is to visit that bygone era. Tales of the theater's construction read like a Verdi libretto. The theater now sees La Sala's balcones and palcos fill up every night, as they have for more than 100 years.

Façade of Teatro Colón

🍴 Grab a cappuccino and dessert at **El Petit Colón** confitería *(see p57)*.

- Map P5
- Cerrito 628
- 4378-7100
- Adm (varies)
- English-language tours every 15 minutes from 9am until 5pm (reservations strongly recommended); tour AR$110 (foreign currency not accepted)
- www.teatrocolon.org.ar

Top 10 Features

1. Entrance Hall
2. El Salón de Bustos & El Salón Dorado
3. Official Boxes
4. Vitreaux
5. La Sala
6. El Paraíso
7. Library
8. La Cúpula
9. Pasaje de los Carruajes
10. Workshops

Entrance Hall

Neo-Romanesque colonnades and a dazzling Belle Époque stained-glass dome distinguish the Colón's entrance hall *(below)*. Four kinds of European marble were employed in the foyer's construction, indicating how highly prized Old World materials and craftsmanship were in the design.

El Salón de Bustos & El Salón Dorado

Busts of Wagner, Rossini, and Beethoven keep watch over theatergoers passing in the entrance hall below. The Golden Salon is Versailles-worthy Baroque. Chamber-music concerts and special exhibitions are held here.

Official Boxes

Reached via El Salón de Bustos, these *palcos* are reserved for dignitaries, the president, and the municipal governor. Most *porteños* say that much politicking occurs in these boxes, which are accessible to the public on guided tours.

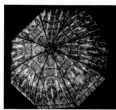

Vitreaux
The massive *vitreaux* *(above)* in the entrance hall is impressive, but do not miss the pair in El Salón Dorado, depicting Greek mythology.

La Sala
There is no such thing as a bad seat within the Colón's auditorium, where upward of 2,500 spectators *(right)* seated in red velvet seats are treated to acoustics only afforded by a theater with the optimal horse-shoe shape.

El Paraíso
The cheapest "seats" also happen to boast some of the best acoustics. Here, in the ironically named Paraíso (Paradise), more than 500 standing audience members can pack in. Optimal sight lines, however, are guaranteed only for early arrivals.

Library
El Colón's formidable archives, accessible to all, contain first-edition librettos, artifacts from past performances, and rich ballet and opera reference materials. The library's main attraction is its complete set of programs from theater performances, dating from its 1908 opening.

La Cúpula
A 3,423-sq ft (318-sq m) dome above La Sala's floor forms the crown on el Colón *(left)*. Its original paintings deteriorated – the present ones were rendered in the 1960s.

Pasaje de los Carruajes
At the top of the entrance hall stairs is this narrow hallway where, prior to the automobile's popularization in Buenos Aires, carriage drivers would pick up and drop off their affluent charges.

Workshops
In the three basements, artisans construct sets, sew costumes, and design props. Performers hold rehearsals on the replicated stage *(right)*.

A Fraught Opening Act

The Colón's cornerstone was laid in 1889, yet the theater would not open for two decades. The lead architect died during construction, leaving his assistant in charge until his own death in 1904, followed by the chief financier's assassination. A Belgian then inherited the project, imparting many French Baroque touches. Verdi's *Aida* finally inaugurated the house in 1908.

Avenida de Mayo

From its inception, Avenida de Mayo was an emphatic statement to the world that Buenos Aires was a cosmopolitan city. The Parisian-style boulevard, lined by uncharacteristically wide sidewalks, links the National Congress to the Casa Rosada, breaking midway at 9 de Julio. While today's mundane shops and stores do their best to diminish the grandeur, Avenida de Mayo's buildings can render even a casual architecture buff mute. Belle Époque, Art Nouveau, and Art Deco façades in varying states of repair coalesce into a textbook study of late-19th- and early-20th-century forms. Some of Buenos Aires' oldest bars, cafés, and bookstores are here, while underfoot, polished teak cars rattle along the city's oldest subway, the Línea A.

Casa de la Cultura

🕐 The Avenida is just 13 blocks, making for a relaxed stroll.

🍽 Stop at Café Iberia (cnr Avda. de Mayo and Calle Salta) for tortilla *española*.

- Map E2
- Hotel Chile: Avda. de Mayo 1297; 4383-0363
- Palacio Barolo: Avda. de Mayo 1370; 4383-1065; www.pbarolo.com.ar
- Hotel Castelar: Avda. de Mayo 1152; 4383-5000; www.castelarhotel.com.ar
- Café Tortoni: Avda. de Mayo 825; 4342-4328; www.cafetortoni.com.ar
- Café Los 36 Billares: Avda. de Mayo 1265–71; 4381-5696
- Palacio Vera: Avda. de Mayo 769–777; 4345-8800
- Teatro Avenida: Avda. de Mayo 1220; 4381-0662; www.balirica.org.ar
- Casa de la Cultura: Avda. de Mayo 575; 4323-9669

Top 10 Features

1. Edificio la Inmobiliaria
2. Hotel Chile
3. Palacio Barolo
4. Hotel Castelar
5. Café Tortoni
6. Café Los 36 Billares
7. Palacio Vera
8. Teatro Avenida
9. Edificio Drabble
10. Casa de la Cultura

1 Edificio la Inmobiliaria

Built in 1910, this distinguished building *(above)* of the Plaza de los Dos Congresos takes its design from the Italian Neo-Renaissance movement.

2 Hotel Chile

Painted brilliant white and accented by gold and blue mosaic tiles, Hotel Chile *(right)* is rhapsodically Art Nouveau. It puts on its best face on the outside.

3 Palacio Barolo

This ornate building, built in 1923, was the tallest until the Kavanagh's *(see p34)* completion in 1935. Its lobby has vaulted ceilings, gargoyle motifs, intricately patterned floor tiles, and wrought-iron elevator cages.

Hotel Castelar
Its name flows elegantly across its awning, an emblem of the Avenida's bygone elegance. The Castelar (above), which opened in 1929, lodged the Spanish novelist Federico García Lorca.

Café Tortoni
The Tortoni (right) offers tango, coffee, and conversation. It is the city's oldest café, having opened in 1858, and is intrinsic to any discussion of the city's lore (see p26).

Café Los 36 Billares
36 Billares (center) is an 1894 dandy, sporting a Movado clock, rich wood paneling, and a billiards hall, thick with smoke and ambience. It offers great coffee, tango shows, and lessons.

Palacio Vera
In this Avenida building's lobby, visitors can gawk at the sixth-story glass vitreaux and delicate molding. El Túnel and El Ventanal are two of the most evocative vintage bookstores in town.

Teatro Avenida
The Teatro Avenida (right) was founded in 1908 to promote the Spanish light opera tradition of the zarzuela. Following a fire in 1979, it was restored to its old splendor and reopened in 1994.

Edificio Drabble
The 1893 Edificio Drabble once housed the upscale hotel Chacabuco Mansions. Today, its crumbling balconies and Mansard roof are reminders of the city's temperamental fortunes.

Casa de la Cultura
Casa de la Cultura, former home of the newspaper La Prensa, is pure Neo-Baroque. The culture ministry desk inside offers a program of the cultural events in the city.

New Avenue, New Attitude

Avenida de Mayo was Buenos Aires' first fully planned boulevard, a project whose scale and expense had never before been imagined on the continent. Torcuato de Alvear (see p59) referenced Paris' Belle Époque-spawned urban planning in the 1880s, but by the time architects started building, Art Nouveau was the rage, resulting in the present structure.

Non-guests can take advantage of Hotel Castelar's renowned day spa (open 11am–8pm Mon–Sat, closed Sun).

Museo Nacional de Bellas Artes

The outstanding National Museum of Fine Arts was founded in 1896 as part of a drive to inculcate a taste for the arts in Argentina. It moved to its present location in 1932, and today preserves over 12,000 works of art. Around 800 of these are in permanent collections boasting the greatest gathering of international masters in Latin America. On display are works by Rubens, Rembrandt, Goya, Rodin, Monet, Renoir, Cezanne, Van Gogh, Picasso, Kandinsky, Pollock, Miró, and Rothko. Argentinian greats to look out for here include Cándido López, Antonio Berni, Benito Quinquela Martín, and Guillermo Kuitca.

MNBA Poster

Exterior of MNBA

🎧 Hand-held audio guides in Spanish and English can be rented from the gift shop on the ground floor, which also stocks excellent written guides to the museum.

🍴 Located behind the museum, the sleek Modena Design restaurant has tasty snacks and a full menu, plus an outside terrace.

- Map N3
- Avda. del Libertador 1473
- 4801-3390
- Open 12:30–8:30pm Tue–Fri; 9:30am–8:30pm Sat & Sun
- www.mnba.org.ar
- Modena Design: Avda. Figueroa Alcorta 2220/70; 4809-0567

Top 10 Features

1. Hirsch Collection
2. Francisco de Goya y Lucientes
3. Graphic Arts 1940–70
4. Pre-Columbian Andean Textiles
5. Di Tella Collection
6. Quirós' Collection
7. 1960s Argentinian Art: The New Figuration
8. Sculpture Patio
9. Mercedes Santamarina Collection
10. 1970s Argentinian Art: Realism

1 Hirsch Collection

Located within the Old Masters wing, this collection features 16th- and 17th-century Dutch and Flemish artists, including works by Rubens and Rembrandt; the latter's *Portrait of the Artist's Sister (above)* is a brilliant study in light and shade. A French tapestry from 1627 and a stunning Venetian Neptune bronze complete the salon.

2 Francisco de Goya y Lucientes

Goya's oil paintings (1808–12) of the Napoleonic Wars depict battlefield scenes in desolate black-gray landscapes, lit only by the orange and red of fire and bloodletting *(below)*.

➡ *If pushed for time, head straight for the stunning modern masters' exhibits – turn right at the main entrance hall.*

Graphic Arts 1940–70

Socialist artists in the 1960s revived engraving in Argentina. Antonio Berni was its greatest exponent. His innovative 3-D technique is seen in *The Bullfighter (above)*.

Pre-Columbian Andean Textiles

Shawls, ponchos, and headdresses here date from the Nazca (0–600 AD) and Chancay (900–1476 AD) cultures of modern-day Peru *(right)*.

Di Tella Collection

Spread throughout the museum, this collection finds best expression in the European avant-garde and American abstract art sections.

Quirós Collection

Cesáreo Bernaldo de Quirós' paintings idealize the wild gaucho as the final stand against modernization and urbanization. *The Butcher* and *Don Juan Sandoval, the Boss (below)* are iconic.

1960s Argentinian Art: The New Figuration

In 1961, four Argentinian artists depicted social breakdown and individual alienation. The fragmented forms in their works replace unity with chaos.

Sculpture Patio

Naturalistic sculptures *(right)* by Argentinian artists girdle the museum's terrace, where the contours of Pedro Zonza Briano's *Be Fruitful and Multiply* ooze sensuality.

Mercedes Santamarina Collection

Pastels by Degas and bronzes sculpted by Rodin are the highlights here. Ming-dynasty ceramics and paintings by Renoir and Cezanne complete this collection.

1970s Argentinian Art: Realism

In the 1970s, Argentinian artists addressed the horrors of the Junta years. Segui's *The Distance of the Gaze* portrays desolation. Heredia's *The Gaggings* expresses terror and censure via absent screams.

Museum Guide

The museum's permanent collections are set chronologically across three floors. The first floor displays international art from the Middle Ages to the 20th century; the second floor, Argentinian art from the 19th and 20th centuries, and Latin American art; the third floor, photography and sculpture. A ground level pavilion hosts temporary exhibitions.

San Telmo

The heart of colonial Buenos Aires, lovely San Telmo is the city's most romantic neighborhood with its cobblestone streets, colonial houses, Spanish churches, and antiques stores. It was first inhabited by elite families who fled during a yellow fever outbreak in 1871, their mansions becoming tenement houses or conventillos for poor European immigrants. San Telmo soon became a melting pot of cultures, a working-class stronghold, and later, a Bohemian quarter synonymous with tango. Newly fashionable and sprinkled with slick loft apartments, chic restaurants, and boutique hotels, it retains an engagingly gritty feel.

Antique jar

Street market, San Telmo

There are numerous places to watch tango in San Telmo. El Viejo Almacén *(see p45)* and Bar Sur (Estados Unidos 299; 4362-6086) are two of the best.

A great place for a snack is El Federal *(see p57)*, a bar-café.

- Map F4
- Feria de Antigüedades: Open 10am–5pm Sun
- Museo de Arte Moderno: Avda. San Juan 350; 4393-2170; www.museodearte moderno.buenosaires. gob.ar; 4342-2970
- Street performers: Calle Defensa btwn Plaza Dorrego & Avda. Belgrano
- Mercado de San Telmo: Calle Carlos Calvo and Bolívar
- Iglesia Nuestra Senora: Avda. Humberto Primo 378
- Pasaje la Defensa: Defensa 1179

Top 10 Features

1. Plaza Dorrego
2. Feria de Antigüedades
3. Parque Lezama
4. Monumento del Canto al Trabajo
5. Museo de Arte Moderno
6. Street Performers
7. Mercado de San Telmo
8. Balconies
9. Iglesia Nuestra Señora de Belén
10. Pasaje de la Defensa

Plaza Dorrego

At the heart of San Telmo, picturesque Plaza Dorrego dates from the colonial period and is ringed by antiques stores, old tango bars, and sepia-toned cafés.

Parque Lezama

A popular recreation area, this park *(right)* is believed to be the spot where Buenos Aires was founded. A statue of the city's founder, Pedro de Mendoza, stands at the park's northwestern corner.

Feria de Antigüedades

This Sunday antiques fair *(left)* has been taking place on Plaza Dorrego since 1970. Items range from 19th-century Art-Nouveau ornaments to the kooky and kitschy. Rummage around for a bargain.

The no. 29 bus line connects San Telmo to La Boca. On its return it descends Calle Defensa, stopping at Plaza Dorrego (except Sun).

4 Monumento del Canto al Trabajo

A muscular allegory of the collective worker, this iconic monument *(above)* depicts workers bound together in hard labor. Facultad de Ingeniería is nearby.

5 Museo de Arte Moderno

At the center of San Telmo's art scene, the MAMBA displays modern Argentinian art, including work by Xul Solar and Antonio Seguí.

6 Street Performers

On Sundays, bands *(above)* cram the sidewalks of Calle Defensa while dancers perform on the cobblestone path. Tango is a big draw here.

7 Mercado de San Telmo

This 1890s indoor market *(below)* retains its original structure. Food and meat stalls occupy the central patio, while knick-knacks are in the outer spaces.

8 Balconies

San Telmo's antique balconies *(below)* range from wrought iron to balustraded stone and span several styles. Many are hung with laundry or bird cages, offering a glimpse into San Telmo's working class.

9 Iglesia Nuestra Señora de Belén

Built in 1733, this church has a Neo-Baroque façade and Andalusian towers, which were added in 1852. The interior reflects the church's colonial origins, with nine altars and saints' statues.

The Founding of Buenos Aires

In 1536, Spanish explorer Pedro de Mendoza led an expedition to the River Plate. He built a settlement at Parque Lezama, calling the town Nuestra Señora Santa María del Buen Aire. Faced with attack from the natives, the settlement was abandoned in 1541 *(see p42).*

10 Pasaje de la Defensa

This residence built for the Ezeiza family in 1872 later became a *conventillo* housing over 30 immigrant families at a time. Today it is home to a colorful flea market.

If you have only one day to enjoy San Telmo make it a Sunday, when the famous antiques fair takes place.

⟨TOP 10⟩ Avenida 9 de Julio

Though it appears as integrated into the cityscape as the rubber trees and crumbling sidewalks, the 460-ft (140-m) wide, 12-lane Avenida 9 de Julio is among the city's youngest public works, having reached its current length – from Avenida Alem to Plaza Constitución – only in 1980. Thousands were displaced when the project broke ground in 1937. The grand houses and churches, including the 18th-century San Nicolás cathedral, became landfill. To their credit, the planners designed a plazoleta-peppered thoroughfare that showcases public art and some of the city's prime attractions. Still, traffic moves at a breakneck pace, conversation gets swallowed by noise, and the Avenida's width does not let pedestrians cross in one traffic-signal cycle.

Calle Lavalle

🚶 Take a detour down the curving Calle Arroyo to glimpse Retiro's most sophisticated street.

🍷 Treat yourself to a glass of Malbec at Winery *(Avda. del Libertador 500; 4325-5200).*

• Map P6
• French Embassy: Calle Cerrito 1399; 4515-7030; open 10:30am–5pm Tue–Fri, 1:30–6pm Sat & Sun
• Estación Constitución: Cnr Calles Lima & Brasil; 4304-3165; open 24 hours; keep watch on cameras and purses
• Museo de Arte Hispanoamericano: Calle Suipacha 1422; 4327-0272; open 2–7pm Tue, 11am–7pm Sat & Sun; adm AR$1 (free Thu); www.museos. buenosaires.gov.ar/ mifb.htm

Top 10 Features

1. El Obelisco
2. French Embassy
3. Teatro Colón
4. Estatua del Quijote
5. Ex-Ministry of Public Works
6. Estación Constitución
7. Calle Lavalle
8. Museo de Arte Hispanoamericano Isaac Fernández Blanco
9. Mansión Alzaga Unzué
10. Plazoleta Cataluña

El Obelisco

This monument *(right)* commemorates the 400th anniversary of the capital's founding and is the site for concerts, performances, and rallies.

French Embassy

Slated for demolition under the Avenida's original blueprints, the fine 1913-Belle Époque-styled French Embassy *(above)* was spared after protests.

Teatro Colón

The Colón *(right)* is an engineering marvel. Its wonderful wrought iron and glass-covered workshops jut out from the main building *(see pp12–13).*

4 Estatua del Quijote

Miguel Cervántes' grandiose anti-hero Don Quixote is cast here in mid-gallop in dramatic bronze on a white stone base.

5 Ex-Ministry of Public Works

This hulking 1936 federal building was the only Avenida structure spared demolition besides the French Embassy.

6 Estación Constitución

After a six-year restoration, this 1887 Beaux Arts structure *(above)* is the city's grandest train station.

7 Calle Lavalle

Lavalle's eastern section is lined with bingo parlors, second-run movie houses, and chintzy restaurants. It exudes a gaudy charm, especially after nightfall.

8 Museo de Arte Hispanoamericano Isaac Fernández Blanco

This Neo-Colonial style mansion *(above)* houses the Fernández Blanco collection of colonial Latin American ecclesiastical art and antiquities.

9 Mansión Alzaga Unzué

The Louis XIII-style Alzaga Unzué *(left)*, built in 1919 for an aristocratic *porteño* family, is today an annex of the Four Seasons hotel *(see p112).*

10 Plazoleta Cataluña

Plazoleta Cataluña is distinguished by a Rambla-style fountain lamp gifted by Barcelona's governors and French chateau-style *tromp l'oeil* treatment.

An Avenida Amble

Start at the Obelisco and move northward up Carlos Pellegrini. Take a tour or check out performances at the Teatro Colón, followed by a bite at the Petit Colón confitería *(see p57).* Walk beyond the French Embassy to the Plaza Cataluña before heading into Recoleta along Avenida Alvear.

🔟 Museo de Arte Latinoamericano de Buenos Aires (MALBA)

Almost at the same time as the collapse of the Argentinian economy, a vital new pillar of national culture rose in Palermo Chico. Since September 2001 the Costantini Collection, a previously nomadic cache of more than 500 prized Latin-American artworks, has lodged in the modern, airy, multilevel institution known as MALBA. Like New York's Museum of Modern Art, the building has been accused of diminishing its paintings, sculptures, recordings, and photographs. Yet visitors strolling through the permanent collection or taking in an art-house film find the scale surprisingly intimate.

MALBA's façade

🚶 English-language guided tours are available for groups who make a reservation in advance.

🍴 MALBA's restaurant serves international fare in a bright, modern setting. Paseo Alcorta's *(see p39)* food court offers dozens of lunch options too.

• Map M2
• Avda. Figueroa Alcorta 3415 • 4808-6500
• Open noon–8pm Thu–Mon; noon–9pm Wed; closed Tue
• MALBA's Restaurant: open 9am–9pm Sun–Wed; 9am–1pm Thu–Sat
• Adm AR$30 (AR$15 on Wed)
• www.malba.org.ar

Top 10 Features

1. Tiendamalba
2. Xul Solar – Pareja (1923)
3. Pablo Curatella Manes – El Acordeonista (1922)
4. Antonio Seguí – La Distancia de la Mirada (1976)
5. MALBA Cine
6. Guillermo Kuitca – Various Pieces
7. Fernando Botero – Los Viudos (1968)
8. Antonio Berni – Manifestación (1934)
9. Ernesto Deira – Nine Variations Over a Well-Tensed Canvas (1965)
10. Frida Kahlo – Autoretrato con Chango y Loro (1942)

Tiendamalba

MALBA's gift shop stocks the requisite post-cards and books, but what sets Tiendamalba apart are its plush dolls, leather cow figurines, and knick-knacks *(below)*.

Xul Solar – Pareja (1923)

Wildly imaginative Solar *(see p88)* is at the height of his powers with *Pareja (below)*. The warmth and light he achieved earned him many comparisons to European masters.

Entrance

Pablo Curatella Manes – El Acordeonista (1922)

This 20th-century sculptor befriended Cubism god-father Juan Gris while in Paris in the 1920s. The Spaniard's influence is seen in *El Acordeonista.*

MALBA Cine

5 From Thursday to Sunday, the city's cineastes descend on MALBA to take in international art-house, cult-classic, and domestic films *(left)*. MALBA's programmers include some Abbot and Costello comedies amid the Jean-Luc Godard thought pieces.

Antonio Seguí – La Distancia de la Mirada (1976)

4 Antonio Seguí, a native of Córdoba, injects a bit of humor into his otherwise dystopian graphite and oil pieces. On a background of gray planes, *la Mirada's* English bulldog gazes out at the viewer indifferently.

Guillermo Kuitca – Various Pieces

6 Having occupied the Argentinian Pavilion at the Venice Biennale in 2007 and worked in a wide range of media, Kuitca is the most famous in the contemporary art scene *(below)*.

Key

▉	First floor
▉	Second floor
▉	Third floor

Fernando Botero – Los Viudos (1968)

7 Fernando Botero might today be known for his controversial *Abu Ghraib* painting series but his legacy are the rotund figures in *Los Viudos* and other similar works.

Antonio Berni – Manifestación (1934)

8 Berni was a great proponent of social realism. Evident in *Manifestación (below)* is his previous dabbling in surrealism.

The New Argentinian Avant-Garde

Paradoxically, the period following the 2001–2002 economic crisis saw Buenos Aires' commercial art scene explode. Artists retreated to La Boca, Almagro, and Barracas' decrepit homes and warehouses to produce aesthetic responses – often mixed-media and digital art – to the chaos befalling their country.

Ernesto Deira – Nine Variations Over a Well-Tensed Canvas (1965)

9 Occupying nine canvases on an entire wall, this work's subtext exalts in, and questions, chaos.

Frida Kahlo – Autoretrato con Chango y Loro (1942)

10 Mexican Surrealism is represented in this self-portrait containing two of Kahlo's favorite motifs – birds and monkeys.

Colonia del Sacramento, Uruguay

Neither the world's widest river delta nor a sovereign border can distance Colonia del Sacramento, or simply "Colonia," from Buenos Aires' orbit. Modern ferries departing from Puerto Madero whisk passengers (with passports) across. Pesos circulate freely among the local currency, the uruguayo, as do wisps of woodsmoke carrying the aroma of grilled beef. But it is the contrasts between Buenos Aires and this UNESCO-recognized, former Portuguese maritime stronghold, established in 1680, that make Colonia worth a visit. Whereas the Río de la Plata is hidden from Buenos Aires' view, it is everywhere here, lapping sandy beaches, reflecting the peninsula's emblematic lighthouse, and swallowing the setting sun.

El Portón de Campo

🚗 Arrive at Buquebus' Puerto Madero terminal at least an hour before departure, as check-in lines can be formidable, especially on weekends.

🍴 Food is prepared uniformly well in the the historic district's kitchens, but for a menu and decor as eclectic as anything in Palermo Viejo, visit El Drugstore *(see p99).*

• Map B4
• Museums: open 11:15am–4:45pm daily; museum pass: $50 (Uruguay); pass can be bought at the Museo Municipal on the Plaza Mayor. It grants access to all seven museums of Colonia. The Lighthouse is not included in this pass.

Top 10 Features

1. Plaza Mayor
2. Museo Portugues
3. El Faro & Convento de San Francisco
4. Real de San Carlos
5. Casa Nacarello
6. Playa Ferrando
7. Iglesia Matriz
8. Calle de los Suspiros
9. El Portón de Campo
10. Rambla Costanera

Plaza Mayor
The Plaza Mayor *(above)* has stately palms and colonies of Austral parrots. Ringed by many museums, it makes a good starting point for exploring the peninsula's cobbled streets.

Museo Portugues
This 1720 bi-level house explores the legacy of Portugal in Colonia. The museum contains 16th-century navigation map replicas, period uniforms, and an intriguing exhibit on the delta's role in the African slave trade, along with artifacts from the period.

El Faro & Convento de San Francisco
The 1857 lighthouse *(below)* pulls off the neat trick of incorporating the ruins of a late 17th-century convent into its form.

For beach trips or a visit to Real de San Carlos, take an ABC bus from Avda. General Flores. You can also take a taxi or a scooter.

Real de San Carlos

This once-grand resort complex is a skeleton of its former self. The Moorish-style bullring *(above)*, casino, and coastal dock, are today a few wooden pilings.

Casa Nacarello

This house *(right)* is a typical mid-18th-century Portuguese residence, stocked with originals and replicas of period furniture. The dark kitchen is very striking.

Playa Ferrando

East of the center is Playa Ferrando, the area's most pleasant beach, with shade trees and a nearby grill. It is best accessed via a rental scooter, but a taxi would cost only US$5.

Iglesia Matriz

Built in 1680, Uruguay's oldest church *(below)* is remarkable for its unadorned white stucco façade and twin cupolas, both of them covered in beautiful Italianate tile work.

Calle de los Suspiros

The narrow streets sloping water-ward from the Plaza Mayor are very picturesque, and Calle de los Suspiros, or Street of Sighs, earns its distinction among them.

El Portón de Campo

This Portuguese-built 1745 archway, the City Gate, is the only structure remaining of the original fortification. It feels almost medieval in its form and heft.

Rambla Costanera

This west-facing street *(left)* hugs the waterfront, affording views of adjacent islands. The rocks below are an ideal spot to eat lunch, and are accessible via two stairways leading down from Costanera.

Getting There

Buquebus, which runs the most frequent ferry service to and from Colonia, has its ultra-modern ticket office and terminal at Puerto Madero's northernmost point (Avda. Antártida Argentina 821, 4316-6500; www.buquebus.com). Swift catamarans make the trip in under an hour, but do not allow passengers on deck. For a more leisurely crossing, take the three-hour *Eladia Isabel*, a comfortable vessel that allows deck access.

 Colonia's clocks are set an hour ahead of Buenos Aires' time in summer.

🔟 Tango

Passionate, intense, and soulful, nothing quite sums up vibrant Buenos Aires as beautifully as the dance form that developed here – the tango. Most historians place its genesis in the 1880s at La Boca's Riachuelo riverbank, where Mediterranean, West African, and Eastern European immigrants would – among other things – dance, sing, and play guitar in the neighborhood's bordellos. But it wasn't long before tango captivated the salon culture of Buenos Aires and, later, the capitals of Europe, incorporating instruments like the piano and bandoneón, and florid, intricate dance steps. Today, tango is regarded as a wholly porteño *invention. Experience the lore and heritage of tango as it has evolved in the city for over 120 years.*

Tango musicians

- Confitería Ideal: Map Q6; Calle Suipacha 382; 5265-8078
- Café Tortoni: Map Q6; Avda. de Mayo 825; 4342-4328
- La Nacional: Map D2; Calle Adolfo Alsina 1465; 15-5963-1924
- Zival's: Map N6; Avda. Callao 395; 5128-7500
- Botica del Angel: Map D2; Calle Luis Saénz Peña 541; 4384-9396
- Chiquín: Map Q6; Calle Perón 920; 4394-5004
- Piazzolla Tango: Map Q6; Calle Florida 165; 4344-8201
- Mansión Dandi Royal: Map E3; Calle Piedras 922; 4361-3537
- Cementerio la Chacarita: Calle Guzmán 680; 4553-9338
- Comme il Faut: Map P5; Calle Arenales 1239; 4815-5690

Top 10 Features

1. Confitería Ideal
2. La Nacional
3. Café Tortoni
4. Zival's
5. Botica del Angel
6. Chiquín
7. Piazzolla Tango
8. Mansión Dandi Royal
9. Cementerio la Chacarita
10. Comme il Faut

Confitería Ideal

Suffering from a touch of neglect, yet all the more evocative and romantic for it, the century-old Confitería Ideal *(below)* remains among the city's most vibrant grand salons, with tango lessons on offer upstairs, excellent musician bookings, and great coffee.

La Nacional

The popular Wednesday night *milonga,* or tango night, at this renovated old Italian social club in Montserrat *(right)* has successfully managed to put the neighborly, communal aspects of tango back into play.

Café Tortoni

Tortoni name-checking is a tango lyricist's tradition. The café *(center)* was the "office" for composers and performers of tango's 1920s heyday. It continues to be a spot to dance and hear groups play live.

Zival's
Quite simply, if a tango recording exists, it can probably be found at Zival's *(above)*. Despite the dizzying inventory, the shop caters just as passionately to buyers who have never seen a *bandoneón*, as to lifelong aficionados.

Botica del Angel

This quirky Montserrat museum *(right)* has little alcoves and rooms packed with tango memorabilia, both kitsch and elegant.

Chiquín
Established in 1905, Gardel *(see p28)* once held court in the dining room here. Now tango/dinner shows are staged every night.

Piazzolla Tango
Tango's most daring modern composer lent his name to this luxe tango dinner-show destination in Galería Güemes *(see p39)*.

Mansión Dandi Royal
The city's most unique hotel, Mansión Dandi Royal features three dance salons, where *milongas (above)* are open to non-guests. Its paintings and furnishings evoke tango's glory days.

Solo Tango TV

Anyone with an Internet connection can enjoy Solo Tango, a channel devoted to the music, movies, and lore of tango. Their performance archives are massive and with the rights to all nine of Gardel's films, viewers can often tune in to see Carlitos romancing his way through foreign cities, rural *estancias*, and aristocratic ballrooms *(www.tangocity. com; Channel 71 on CableVision)*.

Cementerio la Chacarita
Legends like Carlos Gardel and *(left)* Osvaldo Pugliese are buried here. A visit is worthwhile for a Chacarita tradition, where you can leave a smoldering cigarette in the statuary hand of Gardel.

Comme il Faut
Comme il Faut *(right)* is known by tango cognoscenti the world over as Buenos Aires' top purveyor of tango footwear. The staff schedule fittings, if they are not free when you drop by.

Left **Gotan Project** Right **Astor Piazzolla**

TOP 10 Tango Artists

1 Carlos Gardel (1890–1935)
"Carlitos" will always be tango's ambassador. This fedora-wearing *porteño* authored hundreds of tales of love lost, punches thrown, and women wooed. The 75th anniversary of his death was commemorated by four countries – Argentina, Colombia, France, and Uruguay.

2 Astor Piazzolla (1921–92)
Master composer Piazzolla brought tango – some would say kicking and screaming – into the jazz age, pioneering the tango-jazz quintet ensemble and turning American bebop masters on to the artform. The mournful *Adiós Nonino* is Piazzolla's most famous composition.

3 Juan Carlos Copes (b.1931)
An influential choreographer, Copes is responsible for bringing the now-integral theatricality into tango shows: knife duels, dockside scenes, and bordello trysts.

4 Aníbal Troilo (1914–75)
"Pichuco," as his fans and fellow musicians called him, was the colossus of the *bandoneón*, the concertina-like squeezebox on which modern tango's intricate steps are patterned.

5 Osvaldo Pugliese (1905–95)
The pianist and composer Pugliese and his orchestras were broadcast over Radio Mundo, a state-run frequency, which brought his music and his communist sentiments to nationwide attention under Perón (see p33).

6 Horacio Ferrer (b. 1933)
Ferrer has done much through his books to document tango's history and forms, but his legendary lyrics – surreal and florid, like the Piazzolla compositions they were paired with – are his real legacy.

7 Azucena Maizani (1902–70)
Occasionally assuming the macho dress of her male peers, Maizani was a fearless vocalist in the tango *canción* of the 1920s and '30s, featuring in films with Gardel and performing on tours that reached as far as New York.

A Juan Carlos Copes show at the Sorbonne

Top 10 Tango Tunes

1. La Cumparsita
2. Por una Cabeza
3. Mi Noche Triste
4. Silencio
5. El Carretero
6. Tomo y Obligo
7. Mi Buenos Aires Querido
8. Volvió una Noche
9. El Día que me Quieras
10. Guitarra Guitarra Mía

La Cumparsita

To the chagrin of porteños, tango's most recognizable melody, *La Cumparsita*, has its origins in Montevideo, Uruguay, where a struggling architecture student anonymously gave the sheet music to a local band director in 1917. It was only after the student later heard his composition when he was in Paris that he understood his folly – having sold the rights to the tune for just 20 pesos.

The Mythical Gardel

Carlos Gardel might not figure as prominently as Edith Piaf or Al Jolson among early 20th-century vocalists, but the Latin songbird commands an Argentinian cult that would put Elvis worshippers to shame. Gardel wedded lyrics about deceit, drunkenness, and Buenos Aires to tango's florid guitar lines. His presumed birthplace is Toulouse, France, where he was born Charles Romuald Gardes in 1890, though some sources suggest Uruguay is his native soil. Undisputed is his upbringing in Buenos Aires' Abasto district, where push-cart vendors and conmen provided ample inspiration for his songs. European audiences, won over by Gardel's charm, helped legitimize tango in the eyes of porteño elites. Gardel died in a plane crash in 1935, a tragedy which only stoked his legend.

A poster featuring tango star Carlos Gardel

8 Casimiro Ain (1882–1940)

Gardel would have never been able to seduce Europe had the dancer Casimiro Ain not been through Paris in 1904, where this Buenos Aires milkman's son captivated audiences with what was then an unknown artform, which he called "tango *criollo*" (earlier tango). Ain, in a later Paris visit, succeeded in convincing the archbishops that tango was not a sinful dance.

9 Carlos Saura (b.1932)

Spanish director and choreographer Saura is most famous for his *Flamenco* trilogy of films – including 1983's *Carmen*, starring flamenco colossus Antonio Gades – but his internationally screened, highly conceptual, and controversial 1998 feature, *Tango*, helped propel the dance's worldwide renaissance.

10 Gotan Project

The bohemian crew of *porteños* and Parisians comprising Gotan Project are practitioners of electronic tango, which fuses sampling and beats from hip-hop and dub with sultry vocals and *bandoneón*. Their first album, *La Revancha del Tango*, is their greatest statement. Similar to a Cockney slang, the group's name is derived from *lunfardo's* jumbling of the word "tango."

Left **The Bombing of Plaza de Mayo** Right **December Riots**

🔟 Moments in History

1 1536: Pedro de Mendoza Makes Landfall

Leading a 1,200-strong expedition, Spanish explorer Mendoza sailed into the River Plate and founded the settlement of Nuestra Señora Santa María del Buen Ayre. In 1541, with its people starving and under attack from the native Querandí, the settlement was abandoned.

2 1810: May Revolution

Buenos Aires led the region's push for independence from Spain. On May 25, 1810, the Spanish Viceroy was ousted by a revolutionary junta. General José de San Martín led the ensuing war. It ended in 1816 with the declaration of independence.

3 1877: First Shipment of Frozen Beef to Europe

The advent of frozen shipping transformed Argentina into one of the world's richest nations. Robust economic growth remodeled Buenos Aires along modern European lines. Parks, plazas, and mansions were built, turning Buenos Aires into the "Paris of South America."

4 1917: Carlos Gardel records Mi Noche Triste

Since the 1890s, tango had been the music of the city's slum dwellers. In 1916 that changed, with Gardel's recording of the first sung tango. This made Gardel a world star and ushered tango into the salons of Paris.

5 1952: Death of Eva María Duarte de Perón

In 1946, Juan Domingo Perón revolutionized Argentina, mobilizing the support of the country's urban poor to forge a new political movement of hegemonic power. His second wife, "Evita," was key to his popularity and achieved saintlike status among the poor. Her death in 1952 provoked such national grief that her funeral was extended by four days.

Eva Perón and President Juan Domingo Perón

6 1955: Bombing of Plaza de Mayo

After 1952, Perón's regime unraveled. Mobs destroyed opposition party offices, newspapers were closed, and the Catholic Church was attacked. In 1955, Perón threatened civil war on his enemies. In the

Preceding pages **Lobby at MALBA**

Diego Maradona

"Liberating Revolution" the Air Force bombed Plaza de Mayo before ousting Perón.

7 1983: The Return of Democracy
The 1976–83 military dictatorship brutalized Argentina. Left-wing guerrilla forces were eliminated and suspected state enemies arrested, taken to secret torture camps, and killed. The country's defeat in the Falklands War in 1983, saw civilian rule return.

8 1986: World Cup Victory
Argentina's 1986 World Cup victory brought glory to a nation struggling to heal the wounds of the military dictatorship. It also produced a national icon: Diego Maradona *(see p58)*.

9 1992: Israeli Embassy Bombing
The bombing of the Israeli Embassy in Buenos Aires left 29 dead. In another Jewish-targeted attack in 1994, the bombing of the *Asociación Mutual Israelita Argentina* (AMIA), a Jewish cultural center, killed 87.

10 2001: December Riots
In the 1990s, Argentina was crippled by foreign debt and a meltdown occurred in 2001. Government restrictions on bank withdrawals lead to mass riots. President Fernando de la Rúa resigned after 27 died.

Top 10 Literary Figures

1 Jorge Luis Borges (1899–1986)
Argentina's great littérateur wrote *Labyrinths* and *The Book of Imaginary Beings*.

2 Adolfo Bioy Casares (1914–99)
A literary giant, his most famous work is *The Invention of Morel*.

3 Victoria Ocampo (1890–1979)
This 1930s intellectual and feminist was the founder of literary journal *Sur*.

4 Tomás Eloy Martínez (1934–2010)
Historical novelist of *Saint Evita* and *The Perón Novel*.

5 Julio Cortázar (1914–84)
This experimental novelist authored the book *Hopscotch*.

6 José Hernández (1834–86)
Author of the epic poem *Martín Fierro*.

7 Domingo Faustino Sarmiento (1811–88)
Author of what is considered to be the first Argentinian novel – *Facundo*.

8 Manuel Puig (1932–90)
Author of pop culture novels, plus *Eternal Curse on the Reader of These Pages*.

9 Ernesto Sábato (1911–2011)
Sábato wrote *The Tunnel* and also compiled *Nunca Más*, the official report into 1976–83 dictatorship abuses.

10 Jacobo Timerman (1923–99)
Prisoner Without a Name, Cell Without a Number chronicles Timerman's own captivity and torture during the "Dirty War."

Tour agency Eternautas (see p105) runs stimulating historical and literary tours (www.eternautas.com)

Left **Canal 7** Center **Biblioteca Nacional** Right **Automóvil Club Argentina**

🔟 Striking Buildings

1 The Kavanagh
An Art Deco sentinel, the Kavanagh is one of Buenos Aires' most exclusive addresses. It was also the continent's tallest building when it was completed in 1936. Its triangular shape, cleaving two streets, is a rarity among existing examples of the form. ◎ *Map Q5 • Calle Florida 1065*

2 Palacio de las Aguas Corrientes
This Victorian palace is one of Buenos Aires' most fun museums, filled with brass faucets, toilets, and other early 20th-century plumbing relics. The Córdoba entrance has terracotta vegetable motifs. ◎ *Map N5 • Calle Riobamba 750 • 6319-1104 • Open 9am–1pm Mon–Fri • Free guided tours (Spanish): 11am Mon, Wed, and Fri*

3 Palacio Barolo
A richly symbolic building, Palacio Barolo riffs on Dante's *Divine Comedy* in its 328-ft (100-m) height, which matches the number of cantos. Its 22 stories match the number of verses in most cantos. The lobby arcade has dragon heads and hellfire motifs *(see p14)*.

4 Biblioteca Nacional
Palermo Chico's biggest architectural achievement is Argentina's main library. The three-million-volume institution was completed in 1992, three decades after work on it began.

Bring along a photo ID to ascend to the building's reading area, which offers staggering views. ◎ *Map N3 • Plaza Rubén Dário, Calle Agüero 2502 • 4808-6000 • Open 9am–9pm Mon–Fri; noon–7pm Sat–Sun • www.bn.gov.ar*

5 Banco Hipotecario Nacional
This is the most confounding façade in the city. The drape of Swiss-cheese concrete is actually a faithful representation of early 1960s Rationalist design. ◎ *Map Q6 • Calle Reconquista 101*

6 Confitería El Molino
Opposite Congress sits this elegant relic of Buenos Aires' café culture, regrettably closed since the 1990s. Named for its Moulin Rouge-style windmill turret, El Molino was also a

Palacio Barolo

popular tango venue and has many of its Italian glass *vitreaux* intact. ◈ *Map D1 • Cnr Avdas Rivadavia & Callao*

Automóvil Club Argentina

The national automotive club's headquarters is one of Buenos Aires' strongest examples of the Officialist style of

Floralis Genérica

architecture and was designed by local architect Alejandro Bustillo. On its lobby level is a small selection of pristine vintage autos, some of which are of historical value ◈ *Map N3 • Avda. del Libertador 1850 • 4808-4028 • Open 9am–6pm Mon–Fri • www.aca.org.ar*

La Rural

This convention center has been Palermo's slice of Pampa life since 1878. Its annual agricultural show *(see p42)* draws exhibitors and audiences from all over the country. It also hosts other events, such as BA Fashion Week; Arte BA, a contemporary art fair; and Vinos & Bodegas, a wine exhibition.
◈ *Map L2 • Avda. Sarmiento 2704 • 4777-5500 • www.larural.com.ar*

Canal 7

The roof of the city's best-known public television station studios is open to the public. The concrete Bauhaus garden poses a counterpoint to the lushness of Plaza de Uruguay, just opposite the avenue. Do take a peek inside, as emerging Argentinian artists occasionally

exhibit their works in the entrance hall. ◈ *Map N3 • Avda. Figueroa Alcorta 2911 • 4808-2500 • Open 10am–6pm Mon–Fri • www.tvpublica.com.ar*

Floralis Genérica

Argentinian sculptor Eduardo Catalano installed the *Floralis* in 2002, single-handedly bringing *porteño* public art into the Information Age. The aluminum and steel flower "blooms" at 8am, closing its enormous petals at dusk, except on public holidays, when the *Floralis* remains in bloom for 24 hours. ◈ *Map N3 • Plaza Naciones Unidas, Avda. Figueroa Alcorta & Calle Austria*

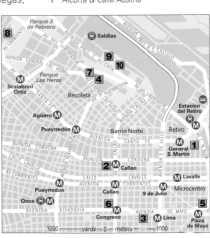

Left **Plaza Lavalle** Right **Parque Las Heras**

🔟 Plazas and Green Spaces

Plaza Rodríguez Peña
Every fall, the lovely flowers of this plaza's tropical jacaranda trees blanket its paths and lawns in a beautiful bluish-purple. It is a picturesque sight and, just one block from the noisy intersection of Avenidas Santa Fe and Callao, a perfect soother for busy shoppers. ◈ *Map N5 • Barrio Norte*

Plaza Lavalle
One of the city's oldest squares, Plaza Lavalle is fronted by important buildings. These include the Teatro Colón *(see pp12–13)* and the Palacio de Justicia (the federal supreme court). The city's biggest synagogue, the Templo Libertad, stands at the square's northeastern corner. ◈ *Map P5 • Barrio Norte*

Plaza San Martín
Named in honor of Argentina's great liberator, General San Martín, this lovely, monumental plaza is sequestered on weekdays by sunbathing office workers and kissing couples. At its center is a magnificent 200-year-old rubber tree, to the east of which stretches a broad balcony with views over Retiro. A memorial to Argentinian soldiers killed in the 1982 Falklands War and a bronze effigy of General San Martín complete this charming square *(see p81)*.

Plaza Vincente López
This lovely plaza recalls the elegant city squares of Paris and London. It is difficult to imagine that it was once a dumping ground for the bloody carcasses of the Recoleta slaughterhouse. Crisscrossed by paths, filled with tropical trees and birdsong, and with beautifully maintained lawns, it is the perfect readers' square. It has a children's play area, too. ◈ *Map P4 • Recoleta*

Jardín Botánico Carlos Thays
Wild and wonderful, the city's botanical gardens combine high art with verdant nature. Opened in 1898 and designed by French landscape architect Carlos Thays, the gardens are home to over 5,500 plant species from every continent. The plant life is interspersed with classical statues and fountains. ◈ *Map L3 • Palermo*

Jardín Botánico Carlos Thays

Watch tango from under a canopy of trees at the Jardín Botánico, which holds free cultural events on weekends.

6 Plazoleta Carlos Pellegrini

This plaza's centerpiece is a striking marble and bronze monument to former president Carlos Pellegrini. Designed by French sculptor Félix Coutan in 1914, it shows a seated Pellegrini flanked by allegories of progress and industry and protected from above by the Republic. ◈ Map P4 • Recoleta

Plaza Serrano

7 Parque Las Heras

At the heart of Palermo, Parque Las Heras is a cool oasis. At its northern end a broad grassy slope descends toward Avenida Las Heras and is a favorite sunbathing spot for scantily clad, sun-worshipping *porteños*. ◈ Map M3 • Palermo

8 Plaza Mitre

This sloping plaza overlooks Avenida Libertador and offers great views across the parks of Recoleta toward Retiro. At the slope's crest stands a monument of Bartolomé Mitre, first president of the Argentine Republic in 1862 and founder of *La Nación* newspaper. Allegorical sculptures adorn its base. ◈ Map N4 • Recoleta

9 Plaza Francia

Facing the Cementerio de la Recoleta, Plaza Francia hosts the city's biggest arts and crafts fair, thronged each Saturday and Sunday by artists and artisans, hippies and neo-hippies, and street performers and tourists. Busiest between 3pm and 6pm, it is one of the city's best free afternoons out. ◈ Map P3 • Recoleta

10 Plaza Serrano

Plaza Serrano, officially named Plaza Julio Cortázar after the Argentinian writer, lies at the center of Palermo Viejo. Petite and circular, the plaza holds a weekend arts fair, where designers display and sell goods. Its perimeter is ringed by hip bars, boho clothes stores, and art studios. Ideal for afternoon and sunset drinks. ◈ Map K3 • Palermo

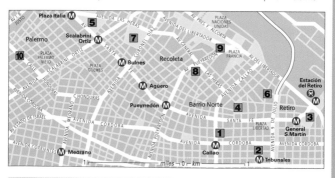

Most of the city's green spaces are open 10am–7pm daily.

Left **Casa López** Center **Plata Lappas shop sign** Right **El Boyero**

Argentinian Artisan Stores

1 Kelly's
In its 50-plus years, this spacious Retiro artisan shop has rescued many visitors from returning home empty-handed. Wares include indigenous-crafted leather items and paintings inspired by the Pampas, but Kelly's is best for *mate* shoppers, with styles and shapes at every price point. 🌐 *Map Q5 • Calle Paraguay 431 • 4311-9189 • Open 10am–8pm Mon–Fri; 10am–3pm Sat*

2 Mission
Resisting the encroachment of Plaza Serrano's fashionable boutiques and fusion restaurants, Mission is pure Pampa. Patchwork cowhide rugs can be custom ordered, and the shop also stocks weathered-wood furnishings, gaucho-style steak knife sets, and leather handbags. 🌐 *Map K3 • Pasaje Russell 5009 • 4832-3285 • Open 11am–7pm daily*

Local craft item on sale in Kelly's

3 Casa López
For many porteñas, Casa López is the only choice for a proper leather handbag. Elegant, handmade designs are offered in a wide variety of styles. Three doors down, at 658, you can find equally luxurious leather fashions, from skirt-jacket combos to full-length coats. 🌐 *Map Q5 • Calle Marcelo T. de Alvear 640 • 4311-3044 • Open 9am–8pm daily*

4 Plata Lappas
Visit Plata Lappas for its exquisite silver pieces, particularly champagne sets and pitchers, plus bone china and silver-embellished longhorn-cattle drinking gourds. 🌐 *Map Q5 • Calle Florida 740 • 4325-9568 • Open 9am–8pm Mon–Fri; 8:30am–1pm Sat*

5 El Boyero
This smartly stocked shop carries Los Robles hide bags and accessories, in addition to crafted gaucho knives, leather wine-bottle harnesses, satchels, and leather footwear. 🌐 *Map Q5 • Calle Florida 953 • 4312-3564 • Open 9am–8:30pm Mon–Sat*

6 Joyería Paula Levy/Viviana Carriquiry
This shared jeweler's space showcases avant-garde silversmithing. Reasonably priced women's necklaces, bracelets, and pendants take on a daring, truly one-of-a-kind form in the artists' workshop upstairs. 🌐 *Costa Rica 4689 • 4833-7430 • Open 11am–8pm Mon–Sat, 3–8pm Sun*

Joyería Paula Levy/Viviana Carriquiry

A belt at Ramos Generales

La Vitrina

Check La Vitrina before other Retiro artisan shops as some real bargains can be had at this no-frills emporium, particularly on woven wall hangings and children's clothing. ✆ *Map Q5 • Calle Marcelo T. de Alvear 566 • 4313-7488 • Open 10:30am–7pm daily*

Estación Sur

Whether it is silver candle-sticks, wooden figurines, or wide-brim leather hats, Estación Sur does them all well, with 300 Argentinian artisans' wares spread over its three levels. The leather, handmade horse saddles are exquisite. ✆ *Map Q5 • Calle Florida 680 • 4328-7189 • Open 10am–8pm daily*

Ramos Generales

Ramos Generales has the most carefully selected artisan-goods inventories in the city. Visit for rich leathers, alpaca-wool sweaters, and hats in leather and traditional gaucho felt. ✆ *Map Q5 • Galerías Larreta, Calle Florida 971 • Open 10am–6pm Mon–Sat*

Joyería Isaac Katz

Isaac Katz works wonders with semi-precious stones, soldering them onto silver rings and into delicate pendants. His wife's contemporary women's clothing line, in the same space, is worth a browse, too. ✆ *Map K3 • Pasaje Santa Rosa 5095 • 4833-7165 • Open 10am–8pm Mon–Sat*

Top 10 Shopping Centers

Galerías Pacífico

Fulfills all domestic luxury brand shopping needs. ✆ *Map Q5 • Linea B Florida 61-62 & 93*

Abasto Shopping

Houses 230 brands, a 12-screen megaplex, a huge food court, and an amuse-ment park. ✆ *Map L6 • Avda. Corrientes 3247 • 4959-3400*

Alto Palermo

This is Buenos Aires' most fashionable place to shop. ✆ *Map M4 • Avda. Santa Fe 3253 • 5777-8000*

Buenos Aires Design

A super emporium of high-end housewares. ✆ *Map N3 • Cnr Avda. Pueyrredón 2501 • 5777-6000*

La Rural

Seek this out for quality gaucho silver knives and leather saddle bags *(see p88)*.

Galería Bond Street

Three levels of skateboard clothing, tattoo and piercing studios, and nightclub-gear shops. ✆ *Map N5 • Avda. Santa Fe 1670 • 4812-8744*

Patio Bullrich

The city's poshest shopping inhabits circa-1860 horse stalls. ✆ *Map P4 • Avda. del Libertador 750 • 4814-7400*

Paseo Alcorta

Four levels of national brands. ✆ *Map M2 • Calle Salguero 3172 • 5777-6500*

Galería Güemes

Home to Piazzolla Tango *(see p27)*, this arcade exudes *porteño* elegance. ✆ *Map Q6 • Calle Florida 165 • 4331-3041*

Galería 5ta Avenida

Buy second-hand vintage clothes and leather-wear here. ✆ *Map P5 • Avda. Santa Fe 1270 • 4816-0451*

Left **Museo de la Deuda Externa** Right **Books on display at Museo Casa de Ricardo Rojas**

Intimate Museums

1 Fundación Forner-Bigatti
This stark white house offers a glimpse into the lives of *porteño* avant-garde artists Raquel Forner and Alfredo Bigatti. Inside, there are sculptures, photos, and paintings in former work-shops as well as the central garden. ◈ Map F3 • Calle Bethlem 443 • 4362-9171 • Call for timings • www.forner-bigatti.com.ar

2 Museo Fortabat
The Museo Fortabat breaks up Puerto Madero Este's tiresome business-park chic with a building as distinctive as its collection of over 1,000 pieces of Argentinian art. ◈ Map R6 • Dique 4

Sculpture at Fundación Forner-Bigatti

3 Museo Casa de Ricardo Rojas
The former home of Argentina's distinguished literature professor appears largely how Rojas left it upon his death in 1957. Its Neo-Colonial design is informed by Rojas' studies of indigenous and Jesuit-mission construction in Peru. ◈ Map M4 • Calle Charcas 2837 • 4824-4039 • Open 10am–6:30pm Mon–Fri, 10am–12:30pm Sat • Adm • www.cultura.gov.ar

4 Museo Histórico de Cera
The passion project of an Argentinian fine arts professor, this wax museum exudes a shabby charm. It features soccer icons, the Revolución de Mayo

(see p32) heroes, literary figures, and more. ◈ Map G6 • Calle del Valle Iberlucea 1261 • 4301-1497 • Open 11:30am–8pm Mon–Fri, 11:30am–7pm Sat & Sun • Adm • www.museo decera. com.ar

5 Museo de la Policia Federal de Argentina
This quirky (some might say creepy) museum begins with a room of eerie mannequins wearing police uniforms. Other exhibits detail activities such as drug use and gambling. The forensics room is not for the faint-hearted; graphic photographs and descriptions of murders accompany the recreation of an exhumed, dismembered body. ◈ Map F1 • San Martín 353 (Upper two floors) • 4394-6857 • Open 2–6pm Mon–Fri

Wax figures at Museo Histórico de Cera

6 Museo de Artes Plásticas Eduardo Sivori

This museum contains a thourough and eclectic array of Argentinian painting and sculpture ranging from the 19th century to the present day. The adjacent sculpture garden is a quiet, contemplative spot. § Map L1 • Avda.Infanta Isabel 555 • 4774-9452 • Open noon–8pm Tue–Fri, 10am–8pm Sat & Sun • Adm; free on Wed & Sat • www.museosivori.org.ar

7 El Zanjón

Rediscovered during a 1980s demolition project, the evocatively lit series of subterranean water tunnels and foundations below El Zanjón mansion have added yet another layer of charm to San Telmo. Check ahead for special events held in the tunnels (see p75).

8 Museo del Cine

Founded in 1971, this institution goes beyond the obvious vintage domestic film-poster exhibitions, putting on in-depth, engaging shows. One such previous exhibition explored early-20th-century Argentinian comic actors' transition from theater to film. The museum also works in tandem with the city's other museums and theaters to screen a range of films. § Map H5 • Caffarena 49, La Boca • 4303-2882 • 11am–6pm Mon–Fri, 10am–7pm Sat & Sun • www.museodelcine.gov.ar

9 Museo de la Deuda Externa

Tucked in the basement of the city university's Economics building, this sober yet absolutely vital mini-museum tracks Argentina's rollercoaster 20th-century economy through 2001's loan default (see p33)

Beautifully lit El Zanjón

with sensational montages and blowups of catastrophic head-lines. § Map N5 • Centro Cultural Ernesto Sábato, Calle Uriburu 781 • 4370-6105 • Open 9am–8pm Mon–Fri • www.museodeladeuda.com.ar

10 Museo Fragata Sarmiento

Named in honor of President D.F. Sarmiento, who founded Argentina's naval school, this 1898 clipper moored at Dock 3 now welcomes visitors aboard her decks. § Map G2 • Alicia M. Justo 980 • 4334–9386 • Open 10am–7pm daily • Adm

Left **Tango in San Telmo** Right **Crowd at Creamfields dance festival**

Festivals

1 Carnaval
A fun celebration of drums and dancing. Each district holds its own parade in which *murgas* (carnival musicians) compete to be the year's best. ✪ *Mid-Feb*

2 Apertura de la Opera
The Teatro Colón, renowned for its excellent acoustics, opens its curtains to opera lovers in early March. The season runs through December. ✪ *www.teatrocolon.org.ar*

3 Buenos Aires Fashion Week
Designers showcase their summer and winter collections at this bi-annual, four-day event, held each March and September. More than 30 catwalk shows take place and 40-plus show-rooms display new designs. ✪ *www.bafweek.com.ar*

4 Festival Internacional de Cine Independiente
This indie-film fest showcases non-Hollywood productions from Argentina and across the globe. Over 12 days, more than 250,000 cinema lovers attend screenings which compete for the *Gran Premio*. Screenings take place daily in locations across the city, along with seminars and workshops. ✪ *Mid-Apr* • *www.bafici.gov.ar*

5 Feria Internacional del Libro de Buenos Aires
This mammoth 18-day fair unites authors and book lovers. Myriad stands sell publications of all genres, and there are seminars and presentations. The likes of Doris Lessing, Paul Auster, Ray Bradbury, and Tom Wolfe have addressed audiences in the past. ✪ *End Apr/start May* • *www.el-libro.org.ar*

6 Quilmes Rock Festival
Past headliners at this four day festival, which takes place at the River Plate Stadium, include acts such as Aerosmith, Ozzy Osbourne, Queens of the Stone Age, and KISS. Buy tickets online as far in advance as possible, as it often sells out quickly. ✪ *Jan or Apr* • *www.ticketek.com.ar*

7 La Rural
The Exposición Internacional de Ganadería *(see p88)* is attend-ed by the farming community from across Argentina and

Opera audience in Teatro Colón

Festival dates sometimes change in Buenos Aires. Check the official tourist website www.bue.gov.ar for latest details.

Buenos Aires Fashion Week

abroad. Exhibits run from hi-tech machinery to GM foods, livestock, and organic produce. The gaucho shows feature amazing feats of horsemanship. ✪ *Late Jul* • *www.ruralarg.org.ar*

8 Festival Buenos Aires Tango
The city's (and the world's) biggest tango extravaganza, this eight-day marathon sees free shows, concerts, classes, and tango fairs take place across the city, before the festival closes with a huge open-air *milonga*. ✪ *Mid-Aug* • *www.mundialdetango.gob.ar*

9 Marcha del Orgullo Gay
Buenos Aires' gay parade is a march for greater rights and a celebration of sexual diversity. The city's gay, lesbian, and transgender communities ride a caravan of glitzy floats in a glorious riot of pink, glitter, and naked flesh to thumping disco and dance beats. ✪ *First Sat of Nov* • *www.marchadelorgullo.org.ar*

10 Creamfields
For dance-music fans, this open-air festival brings together more than 100 artists and 60,000 revelers. Sets feature local DJs with international stars. Paul Oakenfold, Groove Armada, and David Guetta have all played here. ✪ *Nov* • *www.creamfieldsba.com*

Top 10 Contemporary Argentinian Movies

1 La Historia Oficial (1985)
Oscar-winning movie about the fate of the "disappeared" during the 1976–83 military dictatorship *(see p33)*.

2 El Viento se Llevó lo Que (1998)
Comedy in which a village's only experience of the outside is via badly edited movies.

3 Nueve Reinas (2000)
Tale of two grifters looking for their big break in crisis-wracked Buenos Aires.

4 El Hijo de la Novia (2001)
A son whose world is falling apart finds salvation, to his surprise, in his father's love for his ailing mother.

5 Los Guantes Mágicos (2003)
Comedy-drama about a taxi driver confronting loss, loneliness, and crisis.

6 La Niña Santa (2004)
Story of a 16-year-old choir girl's growing sexual awareness and the guilt it provokes.

7 Derecho de Familia (2005)
Funny tale of a neurotic new dad who reassesses his relationship with his father.

8 Bombón el Perro (2005)
Charming road-movie about an unemployed mechanic and his pit-bull terrier.

9 El Secreto de Sus Ojos (2010)
Crime thriller that won the Best Foreign Language Film Oscar in 2009.

10 Los Labios (2010)
Drama about female social workers who visit a poor rural community.

Spanish speakers should visit the website www.cinenacional.com for Argentinian movie reviews and listings.

Left **Salón Canning** Right **Nuevo Salón La Argentina**

10 Tango Clubs and Milongas

1 Centro Cultural Torquato Tasso

This intimate dinner-concert venue is the place to watch live tango performances. Musicians run the gamut from guitarists to accordionists, to flautists, and vocalists such as Adriana Varela – contemporary tango's star. Tango classes precede recitals. Also try the Sunday night *milonga*.
◈ *Map F4 • Defensa 1575, San Telmo • 4307-6506 • Adm*
• www.torquatotasso.com.ar

2 El Querandí

This lively place holds dinner-tango shows in a beautifully restored San Telmo building dating from 1867. Performances are a fusion of tango and theater,

Tango show at El Querandi

telling the story of tango's birth in the city's *bordellos* to its embracement by the bourgeoisie, and later its reinvention by Astor Piazzolla *(see p28)*. The ambience is romantic and intimate. ◈ *Map F2 • Perú 302, San Telmo • 5199-1770 • Adm • www.querandi.com.ar*

3 Tanguería El Beso

This lovely place *milonga* welcomes dancers aged 18 to 80 years, including both tourists and locals. The parquet floor is lit by lantern-like lighting and the horseshoe-shaped bar serves home-made pastas plus wines. Tuesday is touristy, Thursday is

traditional with a smart dress code, while Sunday is the most popular night. Simply choose the night for you. ◈ *Map N6 • 1st Floor, Riobamba 416, Once • 4953-2794 • Adm • Elbesotango@yahoo.com.ar*

4 Niño Bien

This Belle Époque ballroom hosts one of the city's most traditional *milongas*. Here, invitations to dance are made by men only, via a series of nods and signals, and on the floor, dancers locate hands whilst maintaining eye contact – anything else is bad taste. The dance evokes tremendous nostalgia. Expect plenty of tourists.
◈ *Map D3 • Humberto 1° 1462, Constitución • 4883-5426 • Open Mon–Sat*

5 Café de los Angelitos

Opened in 1890, this café earned its "Little Angels" moniker in the 1920s, when it was frequented by the local mafia. Today, it hosts cabaret-style dinner-tango extravaganzas in which dancers perform dramatic and breathtaking tangos to a live six-piece orchestra. Post razzmatazz, visit the bar restored with stained-glass murals and a mosaic floor. ◈ *Map C1 • Avda. Rivadavia 2100, Congreso • 4314-1121 • Adm • www.cafedelosangelitos.com*

 Milongas *are neighborhood dance halls where people go to dance tango.*

Maldita Milonga

6 Come with your dancing shoes on – this *milonga* holds tango classes for beginners and intermediates every Wednesday at 9pm. Live performances include an orchestra and begin at 11pm. ⊗ *Map F2 • Buenos Aires Club, Perú 571 • 4560-1514*

Tango performance at El Viejo Almacén

Salón Canning

7 This elegant tango salon is justly famed for its smooth, polished parquet floor, rated one of the best in the city for tango dancing. Classes and *milongas* pull in a mix of locals and tourists, beginners, and veterans. Monday and Tuesday are the big nights; Thursday mixes tango with salsa. ⊗ *Map K4 • Scalabrini Ortiz 1331, Palermo • 4832-6753*

Nuevo Salón La Argentina

8 The Nuevo Salon has marathon *milonga* sessions on weekday afternoons and on Friday and Saturday nights. It attracts a more experienced crowd that dances *al suelo*, feet pegged to the floor in traditional style with no fancy flicks. The atmosphere is friendly and a bar serves drinks and snacks.

⊗ *Map N6 • Bartolomé Mitre 1759, Congreso • 4371-6767 • Adm*

El Viejo Almacén

9 The setting for dinner-tango shows here is a colonial house. Dance performances are outstanding and feature both traditional and contemporary tangos. There is a six-piece orchestra with violin and accordion solos, a charismatic aging-diva, a silver-haired-gallant, and young-matinee-idol singers. Dinner precedes the shows, and is eaten in a second historical building across the cobbled street. ⊗ *Map F3 • Avda. Independencia y Balcarce, San Telmo • 4307-6689 • www.viejo-almacen.com.ar*

Sin Rumbo

10 It is worth the trip to this outlying *barrio* of Buenos Aires to experience an authentic neighborhood *milonga*. It is best to reserve ahead as the owners close the doors on 150 persons to guarantee plenty of dancing space. The idea is to go for dinner and *milonga*. ⊗ *José P. Tamborini 6157, Villa Urquiza • Adm • www.sinrumbotango.com.ar*

Most tango clubs and milongas offer tango classes. Call for timings.

45

Left **Club Aráoz** Right **Podestá Super Club de Copas** signboard

Nightclubs

Mandarine
International and local DJs spin house, trance, and hip-hop on the main floor in this popular club. The terrace has 80s and 90s pop. ◈ *Map N1 • Avda. Costanera Rafael Obligado, y Sarmiento, Palermo • 4806-8002 • Open from 1am Fri & Sat • www.mandarineclub.com*

Pachá
This 3,000-capacity venue is for fans of techno and electronica. Chemical Brothers, Paul Oakenfold, and Sasha have all played here. ◈ *Avda. Costanera Rafael Obligado, y La Pampa, Palermo • 4788-4280 • Open from 1am Fri, 2am Sat • www.pachabuenosaires.com*

Club Boutique
This club holds the city's biggest "after-office" party on Wednesdays, when people arrive in droves. Dress code is smart. At weekends the music is hard house. The dance floor is overlooked by three balconied levels. ◈ *Map F2 • Perú 535, San Telmo • 4331-6164 • Open 8pm–2am Wed, 10pm–2am Fri & Sat • www.boutiqueba.com*

Podestá Super Club de Copas
Podestá fills with 20-somethings on weekends. Downstairs, DJs spin 80s classics. Upstairs, a more serious crowd boogies to house and techno. ◈ *Map K4 • Armenia 1740, Palermo Viejo • 4832-2776 • Open from 11pm Thu–Sat • www.podestafotos.com.ar*

The Roxy
This century-old theater venue goes glam on Thursday nights when it hosts the city's raunchiest club night, the legendary Club 69 *(see p48)*. Saturday nights are less notorious with Argentinian and international rock and pop. ◈ *Niceto Vega 5542, Palermo Hollywood • 15-4085-5274 • Opening times vary • www.theroxybsas.com.ar*

Full house at Club Boutique

Reserve ahead to dine at most nightclubs from 10:30pm onward – club entry is free afterward.

El Living

El Living is the city's old-school disco for grown-ups. Set across one floor of an old town house, this intimate venue has 80s, disco, and handbag house in the main room and Brit Pop in the smaller lounge. The crowd is an unpretentious mid-20s to late-30s. ✆ Map

Crobar

P5 • Marcelo T de Alvear 1540, Tribunales • 4811-4730

Caix

After Mint or Pachá, the hedonistic head to Caix, the "after hours" club, which keeps going till noon. There is hard techno on the upper floor. The second dance room looks across the River Plate. ✆ Map N1 • Centro Costa Salguero, Avda. Rafael Obligado 1221, Palermo • 4805-6069 • Open from 1am Fri & Sat • www.caix-ba.com.ar

Crobar

It is huge, it is packed, it is Crobar: Buenos Aires' biggest, most popular nightclub, with a mammoth main floor, a smaller backroom, five bar areas, and an open-air terrace, each of which heaves on weekends with an alcohol-fueled mix of tourists and locals. Friday, with the MSTRPLN house night, is the biggie; Saturdays is harder house. Thursday changes tack with US/Brit rock, though in the backroom only. ✆ Map K1 • Paseo de la Infanta, Avda. del Libertador 3883, Palermo • 4778-1500 • Open from 10pm Thu–Sat • www.crobar.com.ar

Kika

A fashionable crowd pours into Kika, which has a cool, flirty vibe. There are two rooms: one hip-hop, funk, and commercial house; the other strobe-heavy hard-house. Sign up on Facebook to get free entry before 1am. ✆ Map J3 • Honduras 5339, Palermo Viejo • 4137-5311 • Open Tue–Sat • www.kikaclub.com.ar

Club Aráoz

Saturday is the big night here, when DJs mix house with reggaetón, hip-hop, and pop. Thursday is hip-hop and Friday rock. The club has an intimacy that the city's super-clubs lack. ✆ Map L3 • Aráoz 2424, Palermo • 4832-9751 • Open from 1am Thu–Sat • www.clubaraoz.com.ar

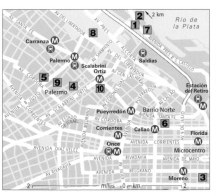

If you are not dining, do not even think about turning up before 2am: it will be just you and the DJ on the dance floor.

Left **Club 69** Right **Gout Café**

🔟 Gay Clubs and Hangouts

1 Amerika
Buenos Aires' biggest gay disco, this venue packs in a gorgeous-looking crowd of gay, lesbian, and straight people. Straights hang out mainly on the top floor, with gays and divas mingling on the lower two levels, where DJs spin techno, dance, and Latin tunes. Expect a night of hedonistic pleasures, even on Sundays. ⦿ *Map K5 • Gascón 1040, Villa Crespo • 4865-4416 • www.ameri-k.com.ar*

2 ZOOM
Located on a corner of one of the city's main cruising zones, this subterranean 24-hour bar attracts an adventurous crowd of Argentinian males and tourists, from 18-year-olds to 50-somethings. Inside is a maze with private cabins and darkrooms. Pre- or post-cruise, chill out in the cool lounge bar, with house beats and flowing drinks. ⦿ *Map N5 • Uriburu 1018, Barrio Norte • 4827-4828 • Open 24hrs daily • Adm • www.zoombuenosaires.com*

3 Club 69
Held in a century-old theater, Club 69 boasts one of the city's wildest club nights, pulling in a mixed gay-straight crowd with hard-house and electronica. The night's big event is a 4am cabaret show, which features leather-clad performers on the main stage. ⦿ *Niceto Club, Niceto Vega SS10, Palermo Hollywood • Open from midnight Thu • www.club69.com.ar*

4 KMØ
This kitschy cool club attracts a mixed gay and lesbian crowd. Highlights of a fun-filled night here include go-go dancers, hot strippers, drag queens, and a huge bar. With a cruise-like atmosphere, the club is at its best on Saturday nights. ⦿ *Map M4 • Avda. Santa Fe 2516, Barrio Norte • 4822-7530 • Open from 11:30pm Thu–Sun • www.kmzero.com.ar*

5 Sitges
This modern pre-clubbing venue crams with an unpretentious gay and lesbian crowd of 18–40 plus. Strippers perform on Friday nights, and comedy drag queens on Saturdays and Sundays. Make sure you turn up before 1am to get a stage-side table. Sitges lacks the cruisey edge of other gay-lesbian venues. ⦿ *Map K5 • Avda. Córdoba 4119, Palermo Viejo • Open from 10:30pm Wed–Sun • 4861-3763 • www.sitgesonline.com.ar*

6 GLAM
Set within a beautiful colonial-style house, Glam pulls in a hip younger crowd of gays and lesbians, especially on Saturdays. There are three bars, a pool room, an exterior patio, a playroom upstairs and, best of all, uplifting dance tunes. The crowd starts coming in around 2am. ⦿ *Map M5 • Cabrera 3046, Palermo • 4963-2521 • Open from midnight Thu and Sat • www.glambsas.com.ar*

San Telmo and Palermo Viejo are Buenos Aires' most gay-friendly districts.

7 Casa Brandon

This multi-level venue serves as a community center, art gallery, bar, restaurant, lounge, cinema, and disco. It's named after Brandon Teena, the transgender teen played by Hilary Swank in the 1999 movie *Boys Don't Cry*. It's primarily a lesbian hangout, but boys and open-minded straight people are welcome too. The atmosphere is casual. ✪ *Map J5 • Luis María Drago 236, Villa Crespo • 4858-0610*
• *Open from 7pm Wed–Sun*
• *www.brandongayday.com.ar*

8 Big One

This mammoth, multilevel venue is housed within a former factory. It throngs on Friday nights when international guest DJs rock the male-dominated dance floors. Handsome, adventurous guys pack out bar areas. There are long queues, so arrive early. ✪ *Map E2 • Adolfo Alsina 940, Montserrat • 4334-0097*
• *www.bigone.com.ar*

9 Gout Café

This gay-friendly café adds a dash of modern chic to the old grandeur of Recoleta. The interior is intimate with modern and elegant decor. The menu features health-food items and a short but high-quality wine list. For afternoon refreshments choose between aromatic coffees, fruit smoothies, muffins, pastries, and brownies. The attractive staff, jazz audio backdrop, and Wi-Fi add to Gout's appeal. ✪ *Map N4*
• *Juncal 2124, Recoleta*
• *4825-8330 • Open 7:30am–9pm Mon–Sat*
• *www.goutcafe.com.ar*

Pride Café

10 Pride Café

This hip café is straight out of New York's Greenwich Village, and is very popular with gay tourists, especially on Sunday afternoons. The menu is completely organic with tasty green salads and delicious cakes and pastries. The cute, friendly waiters are happy to advise on drink options that include coffee, smoothies, or cocktails. The café's interior is a cool, pristine white and chrome affair with a sofa-salon at the back. Outside tables overlook a cobbled street corner. ✪ *Map F3 • Balcarce 869 Giuffra cnr, San Telmo • 4300-6435*
• *Open 9am–9pm Mon–Fri, 11am–8pm Sat, 10am–10pm Sun*

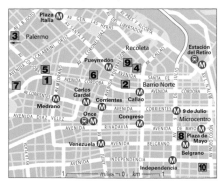

Left **Provoleta** Center **Tourist drinking the ubiquitous *mate*** Right **A box of *alfajores***

🔟 Culinary Highlights

1 Provoleta
The Swiss have their fondue, Mexicans their *queso fundido*, and Argentinians have *provoleta*. An inch-thick disk of cow's or goat's milk (*provolone*) is heated over a grill, rendering it pliant and crisp-skinned. It is eaten with a steak knife.

2 Parrillada
Entrails, sweet-breads, sausages, sirloin, and chicken constitute *parrillada*, brought to the table piled atop a metal grill. You can order the meat *jugoso* (rare), *al punto* (medium-rare), and *cocido* – somewhere between medium-well and well-done.

Baked *empanadas*

3 Dulce de Leche
Most Westerners would recognize the end product of boiled milk and sugar as caramel. Not so in Argentina, where the

Parrillada

ingredients' purity and the heat's modulation yield smooth, shiny *dulce de leche*, doled out with every conceivable dessert.

4 Sorrentinos
Home-made pasta rules in this city, where a third of the population traces its ancestry to Italy. *Sorrentinos,* a staple of the Old Country, are popular in Buenos Aires pasta houses. These round pockets of dough are stuffed with ham and mozzarella, pumpkin and ricotta, or spinach and parmesan, and topped with a traditional cream sauce.

5 Ice Cream
Argentinian ice cream resembles Italian *gelato*. Most *heladería* menus are divided among *frutas* – fruit creams and sorbets; *cremas* – comprising the *dulce de leche* flavors, *sambayón,* and vanilla varieties; and chocolates. If you share a quarter kilo, you get three flavors for US$7.

6 Empanadas
Resembling mini turnovers, *empanadas* are almost always baked – in contrast to their fried Caribbean counterparts – and contain savory fillings such as steak, onion and mozzarella. Keep an eye out for restaurants and

Locro, the local stew

snack bars offering *empanadas salteñas*, *tucumanas*, and *catamarqueñas*, the spicier styles of Argentina's northwest provinces.

Locro

7 A stew from the northwest provinces, *locro* warms you up on cold days. Classic *locro* combines hominy (or corn), meat, and winter vegetables.

Mate

8 Few national pastimes attract such a devoted following as drinking *mate*, the semi-bitter brew sipped at all hours. Hot water is poured on the herb inside a gourd-shaped container and sipped through a filtered metal straw. Try one at Cumaná (see p71).

Fugazzetta Rellena

9 Poke around the pizzeria-clogged intersection of Callao and Corrientes and you will see that *porteños* make pizza their own way. The *fugazzetta rellena* is proof enough – double-crusted pie, filled with cheese and ham, and topped with mozzarella, oregano, and sliced onions.

Alfajores

10 The Oreo cookie of Argentina, *alfajores* can be mass-produced snacks that are available at any kiosk, or handmade delicacies sold at bakery shops. Endless combinations exist, from *maicena* to chocolate-dipped.

Top 10 Argentinian Wines

1 Misterio Malbec
Flichman delivers excellent value within its Misterio line, especially with Malbec, Argentina's prize grape.

2 Pulenta IX Pinot Noir
Production of this Mendoza Pinot, aged 10 months in new French oak, is limited to only about 4,000 bottles per harvest.

3 Telteca Merlot
One of Mendoza's under-the-radar bodegas, its Merlot has tons of fruit.

4 Gran Reserva Malbec
This Malbec is the product of 65-year-old vines and a year of oak aging.

5 Ruca Malen Merlot
On international testers' palettes for a while, this Merlot has fantastic flavor at an unbeatable price.

6 Trapiche Cabernet Sauvignon
From Argentina's most famous winery, this Cabernet is a steal at around US$6.

7 Trapiche Malbec
Argentina's most popular export, next to tango and football stars.

8 Cafayate Torrontés
The white Torrontés grape is province Salta's contribution to Argentinian wine-making.

9 Roble Chardonnay Bodega Los Haroldos
There is nothing subtle about this wine: lots of oak, so it sits well with heavy game and even beef.

10 Bodegas Caro Cabernet Sauvignon
This hard-to-find Cabernet is the effort of the Domaines Barons de Rothschild-Lafite group and a Mendoza family.

 Situated in the west of Argentina, Mendoza is known as land of good sun and good wine.

Left **La Cabrera** Right **Cabaña Las Lilas**

Parrillas

El Desnivel

The archetypal no-frills *parrilla*, Desnivel brims with locals, tourists, and artists. Faded pictures hang on walls and the waiters are the cheeriest in town. Slabs of steak sizzle on the open grill before being whisked to tables. ◈ *Map F3 • Defensa 855, San Telmo • 4300-9081 • Open noon–4pm & from 8pm daily • $$*

El Obrero

Bono, Francis Ford Coppola, and Robert Duvall are just three stars to have joined locals at this atmospheric gem of a *parrilla*, opened in 1954. Hearty meat, fish, and pasta mains are followed by huge, creamy desserts. Service is super-friendly. ◈ *Map H5 • Agustín R. Caffarena 64, La Boca • 4362-9912 • Open noon–4pm & from 8pm Mon–Sat • $$*

La Brigada

The legendary La Brigada combines authentic *parrilla* ambience with first-rate cuisine. The delightful decor has a low timber ceiling and whitewashed walls plastered with soccer memorabilia. Service is super-fast and the steaks are fabulous. Try, too, the delicious *chinchulín* and *molleja* delicacies. ◈ *Map F3 • Estados Unidos 465, San Telmo • 4361-5557 • Open noon–3:30pm & from 8pm daily • $$$*

La Cabrera

A gorgeously romantic spot, La Cabrera comprises two small rooms characterized by bare-brick walls, mosaic floors, and wooden furniture. The steaks are some of the best in town, and the wine list is excellent. Outdoor tables are available as well *(see p93)*.

Don Julio

The chic décor here includes exposed brick and chandeliers, while the specialties are *ojo de bife* (rib-eye steak) and *entraña* (skirt steak). The *empanadas* (stuffed pastries), too, are some of the best in town. Ask for a table on the second floor, overlooking the kitchen below. ◈ *Map K3 • Guatemala 4691, Esq Gurruchaga • 4831-9564 • Open noon–4pm, 7:30pm–1am daily • $$$$$*

El Trapiche

Located in the trendy Palermo district, El Trapiche exudes old-world charm. No extravagant industrial-chic or fancy fusion cuisine here, just

Chiquilín

Parrillas are steak-houses or grill restaurants. To order: vuelta y vuelta (rare), a punto (medium), and bien cocida (well done).

old walls lined with racks of wine bottles, a bustling atmosphere, and a menu that features juicy steaks plus fish, pasta, and seafood favorites (see p93).

Gran Parilla del Plata

This lively steakhouse attracts a healthy mix of *porteños* and visitors, who come for the tasty *entraña* (skirt steak) and *ojo de bife* (rib eye steak), washed down with Malbec wine. Side orders include mash and baked potato with bacon and Philadelphia cream cheese. Book in advance on weekends as it gets very busy after 9pm. ⍟ *Map F3 • Chile 594, San Telmo • 4300-8858 • Open noon–4pm & from 8pm Mon–Sat, from 8pm Sun • $$*

Cabaña Las Lilas

This high-end *parrilla* is famed for its tender grilled steaks. Choose the *ojo de bife* (rib eye steak) signature cut and wash it down with one of 700 Argentinian and imported wines while relaxing within a soothing interior of dark hardwoods and soft leathers. A spacious terrace has lovely waterfront views (see p85).

Chiquilín

Opened in 1927, this famous tango spot breathes tradition. Potted plants, sacks of dry-cured ham, and antique ceiling fans hang from the rafters above a busy main floor that buzzes with the chatter of satisfied customers. On the menu of this traditional and lively restaurant, steaks and pastas make filling mains, and are followed by rich, calorie-charged

La Dorita

desserts. The snappy service adds to Chiquilín's charm. ⍟ *Map N6 • Sarmiento 1599, Congreso • 4373-5163 • Open noon–2am daily • $$$$$*

La Dorita

This atmospheric corner restaurant combines a snug interior with a first-rate grill. The classic *parilla* menu includes a delightful pork-sausage appetizer, a grilled tenderloin sandwich, and the *tables de carne* main in which you choose three of five classic cuts to share between two people. Wash it all down with wine poured from the barrel and served in clay jugs. Outside tables are available, but inside is much more romantic. ⍟ *Map J3 • Humboldt 1892 • 4776-5653 • Open noon–4pm & from 8pm Mon–Sat • $$$*

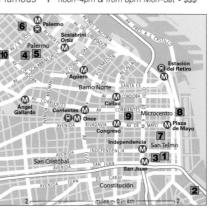

Left **Duhau Restaurante and Vinoteca** Center **Ølsen** Right **La Bourgogne**

TOP 10 Restaurants

1 Chez Nous
The eclectic blend of French and Argentinian cuisine here is made from organic produce.
✪ Map P4 • Montevideo 1647, Recoleta • 3530-7777 • Open 7am–midnight Sun–Wed, 7am–1am Thu–Sat • $$$$$

2 Patagonia Sur
Star chef Francis Mallmann's *prix fixe* menu changes regularly, spotlighting in-season ingredients like *calafate* berries and Andean potatoes. Desserts and wines are stellar, as is the intimate setting (see p77).

PATAGONIA SUR

Patagonia Sur sign

3 Ølsen
The cavernous Ølsen has begun polarizing the *porteño* tastemakers who initially pegged it to the international style map, yet the scene is still there to make: Scandinavian preparations of finger foods, a lively brunch, and an outdoor patio for sipping a vodka cocktail (see p93).

4 Duhau Restaurante and Vinoteca
Extraordinary service, nuanced food preparation, and grandeur are all part of the Duhau dining experience. There is seating in a tranquil outdoor garden, the warmly appointed dining room, or in the *vinoteca* – a comfortable space where cheeses pair up with Malbecs and artisanal breads (see p71).

5 Oui Oui
The bright, airy Oui Oui is one of Palermo's most pleasant surprises. Come for light egg dishes, lemonades, soufflés, tarts, brioches, soups, and savory waffles. It is ideal for a *merienda*, or afternoon bite.
✪ Map J2 • Calle Nicaragua 6068 • 4778-9614 • Open 8am–8pm Tue–Fri, 10am–8pm Sat–Sun • www.ouioui.com.ar • $

6 Brasserie Petanque
This is pitch-perfect French bistro dining. Massive windows open onto Defensa in warm months, making for one of the capital's most boisterous foodie scenes. The daily catch on the specials board is always exceptional, as is the well-selected paté platter for starters. The waiters know their wines and how to pair them too (see p77).

The bar of Brasserie Petanque

Nectarine 2.0

7 Surrender to a memorable gastronomic experience at this handsome French nouvelle restaurant, with its eight- or 10-course menu. The exposed kitchen allows unfettered viewing of masters at work *(see p71)*.

La Bourgogne

8 Chef Jean Paul Bondoux relishes utilizing local ingredients, particularly Malbec wine, in his cooking. Gourmets from the world over come here for the food *(see p71)*.

The interior of Tomo 1

Tomo 1

9 No other restaurant in Buenos Aires delivers on *porteño* cuisine's potential like Tomo 1, founded in 1971. The duck ravioli in fruit reduction, poached Patagonian trout with mint, and passion-fruit mousse justify this restaurant's pedigree *(see p85)*.

Casa Cruz

10 Behind imposing golden doors lies the brooding, opulent Casa Cruz. Delicate, moderate portions of Asian and Argentinian cuisine are nibbled by Buenos Aires' elite *(see p93)*.

Top 10 Cafés and Confiterías

1 El Petit Colón
This is the post-performance drink and discussion spot of the city.
Ⓢ *Map P6 • Calle Libertad 505*

2 Café Tortoni
Tortoni prepares the best *churros con chocolate caliente* in the city *(see p26)*.

3 Pride Café
White walls, modernist lighting, and alfresco frontage distinguish this gay-friendly café *(see p49)*.

4 Bar 6
The daily happy hour (6:30–8:30pm) at this bar/café attracts the neighborhood crowd *(see p92)*.

5 La Biela
Watch people pass by while having your sandwich *tostado* and coffee *(see p70)*.

6 Clásica y Moderna
This part-bookstore and part-café charms with its live piano *(see p70)*.

7 Bar Plaza Dorrego
The coffee is made to order, salads are ample, and waiters are on the charming side of brusque *(see p77)*.

8 Bar El Federal
Order a liquored-up coffee and admire the vintage fixtures. Ⓢ *Map F5 • Cnr Calles Perú & Carlos Calvo • 4300-4313*

9 Bar Británico
Witness the porteño art of making a coffee last two hours in this 24-hour open bar. Ⓢ *Map F4 • Cnr of Calles Brasil & Defensa • 4361-2107*

10 La Americana
Come to this pizzeria for slow lunches, *empanadas*, and *fugazzetta rellena* pie *(see p53)*. Ⓢ *Map D1 • Avda. Callao 83 • 4371-0202*

For price ranges, **See p71.**

Left **Former president Juan Domingo Perón** Right **Jorge Rafael Videla**

Porteño Personalities

1 Diego Maradona (b. 1960)
Known as "El Diez," "El Pibe", "Dios", by his jersey number, as "the kid" or, simply, "God," Diego Maradona is the face of Argentinian soccer. His two goals in the 1986 quarter-final against England are the most infamous and sublime in World Cup history.

2 Carlos Gardel (1890–1935)
"Gardel sings better every day," so goes the refrain in Buenos Aires. Such is the unwavering love for this tango legend, whose singing and songwriting helped break tango worldwide *(see pp28–9)*

3 Susana Gimenez (b. 1944)
Former actress and current talk-show host, Susana Gimenez, though close to retirement age, does not look a day over 35. She can still be seen gracing magazine covers and high-profile social gatherings every week.

4 Carlos Menem (b. 1930)
Former president Menem's tax incentives for foreign investors facilitated Puerto Madero's reinvention in the 1990s. Still, it is his image of being ordered by the Congress to relinquish a Ferrari gifted by businessmen, that has come to symbolize his corrupt presidency.

5 Evita Perón (1919–52)
María Eva Duarte, a Pampas-born actress and dancer, was one half of the Argentinian power couple of the century with General Juan Perón. Her adoring legions called her by the Spanish diminutive "Evita" and her mausoleum in the Recoleta *(see p10)* is never without a bouquet or a crowd.

6 Juan Perón (1895–1974)
Juan Domingo Perón was a pro-working class, populist president who promoted social welfare programs. Also a Nazi sympathizer, he actively aided former SS officers to immigrate to Argentina. Despite his mixed legacy, the political movement with his name is still powerful.

7 Charly García (b. 1951)
Together with Luis Spinetta, Charly García gave rock 'n roll a *rioplatense* accent. After his first band, Sui Generis, dissolved in 1975, Garcia's solo career launched him into *rock en*

Former president Carlos Menem

Porteños are people native to or inhabiting the port city of Buenos Aires.

Author Jorge Luis Borges

español. Now semi-retired, he does occasional live shows, the most memorable being the one on the Madres' 30th anniversary in 2007 *(see p9)*.

8 Jorge Luis Borges (1899–1986)

In death, the laureate of Buenos Aires enjoys as high a literary profile as he did in life. Borges' existential novellas, *The Aleph* and *The Secret Miracle*, are required accessories for any self-respecting philosophy and letters under-graduate.

9 Jorge Rafael Videla (b. 1925)

After the restoration of democracy in 1983, self-appointed president General Videla was in and out of jail, courtrooms, hospitals, and, at time of writing, under house arrest following charges of human rights abuses. *Porteño* street graffiti calls for his retrial.

10 Torcuato de Alvear (1822–90)

If Buenos Aires is likened to Paris, a debt is owed to the city's first mayor, Torcuato de Alvear. He oversaw the urban planning of Recoleta as well as Avenida de Mayo, and began infrastructure projects that facilitated the capital's growth.

Top 10 Argentinian Musical Stars

1 Fito Páez
A piano balladeer, Páez's talents include writing films.

2 Andrés Calamaro
The gritty-voiced Calamaro paid homage to Bob Dylan in 2007 with *La Lengua Popular*.

3 Soda Stereo
The Latin American band of the 1980s and '90s, Soda reunited in 2007 for a tour.

4 Patricio Rey
This artist infused old-rock 'n roll with Buenos Aires slang, or *lunfardo*.

5 La Renga
Adding the metal-tinged guitar to 1980s rock, La Renga highlighted the poverty plaguing the city's *barrios*.

6 Attaque 77
Skater punks Attaque have been the conscience of *porteño* youth for two decades.

7 Bersuit Vergarabat
Bersuit led the *rock nacional* scene of the 1990s and early 2000s, championing drunken anti-heroes.

8 Los Fabulosos Cadillacs
The band's 1994 hit, *Matador*, is still a frequent request, though the singer Vincentico has since found solo success.

9 Gustavo Santaolalla
Santaolalla is a popular Argentinian musician and wrote the soundtracks for *Brokeback Mountain* and *The Motorcycle Diaries*.

10 Juana Molina
Molina, distinguished by her ethereal voice and quirky pop instrumentation, has recorded some of the most critically acclaimed albums of the past decade.

Left **Museo de los Niños** Center **Parque 3 de Febrero** Right **Planetario Galileo Galilei**

🔟 Activities for Children

1 Museo Argentino del Títere

This museum displays antique puppets from countries as diverse as Romania, Indonesia, Costa Rica, and India. Shows are staged on weekends. 🅢 *Map E3*
• *Piedras 905, San Telmo* • *4307-6197*
• *Open 10am–12:30pm, 3–6pm Tue, Wed & Fri; 3–6pm Thu, Sat–Sun* • *Adm for shows* • *www.museoargdeltitere.com.ar*

2 Planetario Galileo Galilei

Educational and highly enjoyable, the daily shows at the city's spaceship-shaped planetarium, take you on a journey through the cosmos, as you sit comfortably beneath a giant domed ceiling. Narrations are in Spanish and English *(see p89)*.

3 Museo Argentino de Ciencias Naturales

The natural sciences museum features dinosaur displays, an aquarium, an Antarctic section, and rooms of amphibians, reptiles, and insects. Have snacks at the "Bottom of the Sea" café. 🅢 *Map J6* • *Avda. Angel Gallardo 470, Caballito* • *4982-6595* • *Open 2–7pm daily*
• *Adm* • *www.macn.gov.ar*

Museo Argentino de Ciencias Naturales

4 Tren de la Costa

This train skirts the Río de la Plata between Olivos and Tigre *(see p96)*. Enjoy river beaches, Rollerblading, and bike-riding en route. The Parque de la Costa and Delta are nearby. 🅢 *4002-6000*
• *Open 6:30am–11pm* • *Adm*
• *www.trendelacosta.com.ar*

River Delta boat ride

5 River Delta Boat Rides

The Delta is a lush microhabitat of water channels and dense islands. One or two-hour boat rides will have you and the kids feeling like Indiana Jones.
🅢 *Launches depart from the Estación Fluvial de Tigre: Mitre 305, Tigre* • *4512-4497* • *Adm* • *www.vivitigre.com.ar*

6 La Calle de los Títeres

This "puppet street" is a popular attraction. Families gather in the courtyard of an 1840s house, where children take part in art workshops before the puppet shows begin. Great for 3–7-year-olds. 🅢 *Map D5* • *Centro Cultural del Sur, Avda. Caseros 1750, Constitución* • *4305-6653* • *Open from 5pm Sat & Sun (closed Jan, Feb)*

Children with camel, Jardín Zoológico

Jardín Zoológico
Snow leopards and Bengal tigers are the stars of this zoo, but other attractions include an aquarium, boat rides, and a farm where children can milk cows, bake bread, and guess animals via sound and texture (see p88).

Museo de los Niños
In this mini-city, kids can shop at a supermarket, work an airport X-ray machine, crawl through waterworks, pilot a plane, film a TV show, and partake in myriad other activities. ✆ Map L6 • Avda. Corrientes 3247, Abasto • 4861-2325 • Open Mar–Dec 1–8pm Tue–Sun • www.museo abasto.org.ar

Parque de la Costa
This popular amusement park has rides from bumper cars to adrenalin-pumping roller coasters. Combine with a Delta boat trip for the perfect day out. ✆ Vivanco 1509, Tigre • 4002-6000 • Open 11am–8pm Fri–Sun • Adm • www.parquedelacosta.com.ar

Parque 3 de Febrero
Float across a lake in a pedal-powered boat or rowboat, rent Rollerblades or a bike, visit rose and Japanese gardens, or ride in a horse-drawn carriage at this lovely park. Combine with a visit to the nearby city zoo and planetarium. ✆ Map L2 • Avda. del Libertador y Avda. Sarmiento

Top 10 Children's Stores

1 Barbie Store
Barbie-themed fashion, toys, beauty center, teahouse, and playroom. ✆ Map M3 • Avda. Scalabrini Ortiz 3170, Palermo • 0810-4444-227243

2 Chibel
Wide selection of kids' wear. ✆ Map J4 • Loyola 770, Palermo Viejo • 4504-8688

3 Imaginarium
Games, dolls, music kits, and more. ✆ Map Q6 • Florida 737 • 5555-8150

4 Viva La Pepa
Handmade designs include vintage-inspired party dresses. ✆ Map J2 • Gorriti 5868, Palermo Viejo • 4776-5213

5 Cheeky
Cute clothes for new borns–12 year-olds. ✆ Map P5 • Avda. Santa Fe 1499, Barrio Norte • 4813-1875

6 Owoko
Fun designs using high-quality fabrics. ✆ Map K4 • El Salvador 4694, Palermo Viejo • 4831-1259

7 Bukito
Well-priced toys, clothes, babyseats, and more. ✆ Map L6 • Avda. Corrientes 2699, Abasto • 4961-1112

8 Mimo and Co
This chain store stocks clothes and accessories. ✆ Map L6 • Avda. Corrientes 3247, Abasto • 4959-3545

9 Super Baby
Browse the collection while kids play with puppets. ✆ Map L3 • Armenia 2302, Palermo Viejo • 4833-6636

10 Gabriela de Bianchetti
Original designs with flowery motifs on exclusive fabrics. ✆ Map K4 • Scalabrini Ortiz 1305 • 4831-6941

Most children's stores in Buenos Aires cater to children aged 0–12 years.

61

AROUND TOWN

Barrio Norte, Recoleta
& Around
64–71

San Telmo & La Boca
72–77

Microcentro, Puerto
Madero & Retiro
80–85

Palermo
86–93

Beyond Buenos Aires
94–99

BUENOS AIRES' TOP 10

Left **Avenida de Mayo** Right **Teatro Colón**

Barrio Norte, Recoleta & Around

A T THE HEART OF BUENOS AIRES LIES *the Plaza de Mayo (see pp8–9),
from which several distinct neighborhoods radiate. Encompassing the
Plaza is historic Monserrat, which is crammed with colonial buildings. Head
north from here and you reach the rich northern neighborhoods of Barrio
Norte and Recoleta. Travel west and you hit the colorful working-class
districts of Once, the spiritual home of the city's Jewish community, and
Abasto, the tango neighborhood that gave the world Carlos Gardel (see p28).
Grand avenues link these neighborhoods to each other. The oldest of them
all, Avenida de Mayo, has stunning belle-époque architecture (see pp14–15).*

Café in Avenida Corrientes

🔟 Sights

1. Avenida 9 de Julio
2. Avenida de Mayo
3. Museo Nacional de Bellas Artes
4. Cementerio de la Recoleta
5. Avenida Corrientes
6. Centro Cultural Recoleta
7. Museo de la Ciudad
8. Teatro Colón
9. Manzana de las Luces
10. Museo Casa Carlos Gardel

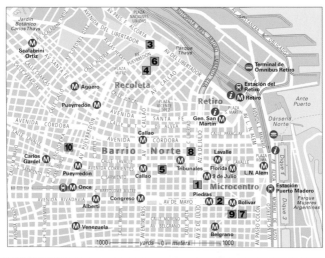

Preceding pages **Fountain at the Congreso Nacional**

Museo Nacional de Bellas Artes

Avenida 9 de Julio

Conceived in the 1930s as a means of alleviating gridlocked north-south traffic in the city center, Avenida 9 de Julio cut a 459-ft (140-m) wide swath from Constitución station to Retiro. The city's youngest public work, this avenue creates a symbolic link between the traditionally working-class southern *barrios* and the aristocratic north, yet the frenetic span in between knows no such distinctions. Along this busy and exciting street, a visitor is as likely to enjoy a slice of 6-peso pizza along its jacaranda-lined flanks as catch a deluxe tango dinner show in a neighboring hotel's ballroom *(see pp20–21)*

Avenida de Mayo

The city's first great boulevard, the grand Avenida de Mayo was built in 1894 to link Argentina's two seats of governmental power – the Casa Rosada presidential palace and the Palacio del Congreso. Fronted by Parisian palaces and cupolas, the Avenue's magnificent architecture is a reflection of Buenos Aires' Francophile pretensions of the time. Ironic, then, that it was the Spanish community who made the avenue its own, lining it with Iberian cafés, restaurants, and bars, most of which are open and very popular even today *(see pp14–15)*.

Museo Nacional de Bellas Artes

Buenos Aires' fine arts museum, the MNBA was founded in 1896 and houses over 12,000 works of art. Permanent collections on display include pre-Columbian art, Argentinian art of the 19th and 20th centuries, and international art by old and modern masters, including Goya, El Greco, Van Gogh, Picasso, Kandinsky, and Miró. An auditorium screens films daily *(see pp16–17)*.

Cementerio de la Recoleta

Explored via a labyrinth of streets and narrow alleys, Cementerio de la Recoleta, the fabulous city of the dead, is the burial place of presidents, military generals, and patrician families of Argentina. Its high walls protect mausoleums of granite and bronze topped by cupolas and marble sculptures of angels and crying mothers. Its most famous resident is Evita Perón *(see p58)*, though the most beautiful tomb is that of José C. Paz *(see pp10–11)*.

Cementerio de la Recoleta

Shalom Buenos Aires

Buenos Aires is home to Latin America's biggest Jewish community, and its hub is the *barrio* of Once. This bustling, colorful, traffic-choked district is lined with Jewish businesses, delicatessens, kosher restaurants, and temples. At its heart is the AMIA building, the site of one of two Jewish-targeted terrorist attacks in the 1990s *(see p33)*.

Avenida Corrientes

The center of the city's theater district, this legendary thoroughfare was called "the avenue that never sleeps" in the 1940s, when it overflowed with theaters and movie theaters. Today, it is a tad bedraggled though the theaters remain. It is also lined with cafés and bookstores, including excellent second-hand stores *(see p69)*.
◈ Map P6

Centro Cultural Recoleta

A vibrant contemporary art space, this cultural center occupies the old Recoleta monastery, built in 1732. Twenty separate galleries host temporary exhibitions. Exhibits are edgy, provocative, and rich in social, political, and religious comment. There is also a micro-movie theater, an auditorium housed in the monastery chapel, several multifunctional spaces,

Centro Cultural Recoleta

Exhibits at Museo de la Ciudad

and a roof-top terrace where performances take place in summer. ◈ *Map N3 • Junín 1930 • 4803-1040 • Open 2–9pm Mon–Fri, noon–9pm Sat & Sun • www.centroculturalrecoleta.org*

Museo de la Ciudad

Housed in a private residence dating from 1894, this museum includes recreations of Art Nouveau and Art Deco bedrooms, a typical 1900s office, and a dining room from the 1950s. Other displays feature antique children's toys, architectural antiques, and period furniture and paintings. The Farmacia de la Estrella in the same block is a functioning pharmacy open since 1834. It includes ceiling frescoes and an antique counter and weighing scales. ◈ *Map F2 • Defensa 219, Montserrat • 4331-9855 • Open 11am–7pm Mon–Fri, 10am–8pm Sat & Sun • Adm*

Teatro Colón

Inaugurated in 1908, the Teatro Colón is one of the world's great opera houses. Opera, ballet, and classical music concerts take place in its auditorium and past performers have included Pavarotti, Nureyev, and María Callas. You can take a guided tour of its majestic interior, auditorium, salons, and labyrinth of workshops and rehearsal rooms *(see pp12–13)*.

Manzana de las Luces

The city's historical heart, Manzana de las Luces (The Block of Enlightenment), is a complex of Jesuit and government buildings dating from the mid-17th century. Highlights include the city's oldest church – Iglesia San Ignacio – built in 1668, the old Jesuits' headquarters, the Sala de Representantes, and the Colegio Nacional de Buenos Aires. Running beneath the block are tunnels built in the 1690s to link this site with the Plaza de Mayo. ◈ Map F2 • Perú 272, Montserrat • 4342-6973
• www.manzanadelasluces.gov.ar

Museo Casa Carlos Gardel

This museum is set within the house Gardel (see p28) shared with his mother in the years prior to his death in 1933. A typical *casa chorizo*, from early 20th-century Buenos Aires, the house displays Gardel's eventful life through the family photos, vinyl records, and movie posters on display. A micro-movie-theater shows Gardel's old movies and a section of the house has been restored to show how he lived. ◈ Map M5 • Jean Jaurés 735, Abasto • 4964-2015 • Open 11am–6pm Mon, Wed–Fri; 10am–7pm Sat & Sun • Adm • www.museocasacarlosgardel. buenosaires.gov.ar

Museo Casa Carlos Gardel

A Day of Monuments

Morning

🕐 Have breakfast at **La Americana** (see p57) before walking east down **Avenida de Mayo**, admiring this avenue's fabulous architecture, in particular the Art Nouveau **Hotel Chile** (see p14) and the Neo-Gothic **Palacio Barolo** (see p14). At the avenue's intersection with Perú, turn right after two blocks for **Manzana de las Luces** and take a thrilling journey back in time to 17th-century Buenos Aires. Continue this historical thread by exploring Manzana's jumble of adjoining streets, popping into the **Museo de la Ciudad**. Return to **Avenida de Mayo** for coffee and croissants at **Café Tortoni** (see p15). Walk west to **Avenida 9 de Julio** (see p65), where you can take a tour of the beautiful **Teatro Colón**.

Afternoon

Head to Recoleta, and take lunch at **La Biela** (see p70). Post-meal, wander the streets and alleys of the **Cementerio de la Recoleta** (see p65), which is directly opposite. Then browse contemporary art at the **Centro Cultural Recoleta**. Head up to the roof terrace here for lovely views. From the **Centro Cultural** cross **Plaza Francia** (see p37) to the Avenida Alvear. Walk three blocks east along Alvear to the **Alvear Palace Hotel** (see p112), where you can stop for high tea. Heading east again, explore high-fashion boutiques before turning right at the intersection with Libertad to end your day with wine and dinner at **Gran Bar Danzón** (see p70).

➡ After visiting the Museo Casa Carlos Gardel, stroll the adjacent Zelaya street, a colorful side-street decorated with tango murals.

Left **Kosiuko** Center **Tramando** Right **Ona Sáez**

🔟 Recoleta Stores

1 Puro Diseño
Housed within the city's mecca for interior design – Buenos Aires Design – Puro Diseño specializes in household products with a modern, innovative twist. 🛇 *Map N3 • Avda. Pueyrredón 2501 • 5777-6104*

2 Tramando
This boutique is dedicated to women's wear and interior design. Collections are super-stylish, handmade, and very exclusive. 🛇 *Map P4 • Rodríguez Peña 1973 • 4811-0465*

3 Kosiuko
Kosiuko stocks funky men's, women's, and children's wear, all at good prices. 🛇 *Map N5 • Avda. Santa Fe 1779 • 4815-2555*

4 Ona Sáez
Sáez's collections feature combat pants, men's evening wear, slinky cocktail dresses, and great daywear. 🛇 *Map N5 • Avda. Santa Fe 1570 • 4815-0029*

5 Vasalissa
Ingredients of the imported Belgian chocolates sold here include passion fruit, champagne, and cassis. 🛇 *Map P4 • Avda. Callao 1940 • 4806-4158*

6 De Maria
Shop here for elegant women's footwear and accessories made from snakeskin, patent leather, and more. 🛇 *Map P4 • Libertad 1655 • 4815-5001*

7 Lulu of London
This exclusive beauty salon's services include waxing, aromatherapy, and massages. Do make a prior appointment. 🛇 *Map N5 • Rodríguez Peña 1057 • 4815-8471*

8 María Vásquez
This flower-filled boutique is the perfect showcase for María Vásquez's gorgeously chic collection, aimed at 20–35-year-old women. The prices are also exclusive. 🛇 *Map P4 • Libertad 1632 • 4815-6333*

9 Celedonio
This jewelry designer handcrafts stunning necklaces in dashing baroque designs, using silver and semi-precious stones such as jade, coral, and river pearl. 🛇 *Map P4 • Uruguay 1223 No. 8 • 4303-7598*

10 Benedit Bis
The Benedit sisters design striking daywear for young women. Designs come in bold colors and light fabrics. 🛇 *Map P4 • Galería Promenade, Avda. Alvear 1883 • 4361-0577*

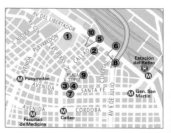

Wherever you shop in the city say the words para regalar and the attendant will happily gift wrap your purchase for you.

Left **Teatro Metropolitan** Center **Teatro Gran Rex** Right **Cadore**

🔟 Avenida Corrientes Highlights

Libreria Losada
This bookstore holds over 50,000 titles covering a wide range of topics. ◈ Map N6 • Avda. Corrientes 1551 • 4375-5001

Rigoletto Curioso
This store sells pop memorabilia and reproductions. Best of all are the antique theater posters. ◈ Map N6 • Avda. Corrientes 1660 • 6320-5310

Zum Edelweiss
This restaurant and beerhouse recalls the 1930s heyday of Avenida Corrientes. It has been run by the same family of German descent since 1933. ◈ Map P5 • Libertad 431 • 4382-3351

Teatro Metropolitan
In an Art Deco building, the Metropolitan stages local productions as well as imported Broadway-style shows. ◈ Map P6 • Avda. Corrientes 1343 • 4373-4444

Bombonella
This chocolatier is great for inexpensive gifts, with big candy love hearts and chocolatey images of national icons. ◈ Map P6 • Avda. Corrientes 1479 • 4371-0633

Teatro San Martín
This state-run theater has superb facilities that include three auditoriums and an arthouse cinema. It holds first-rate ballet productions. ◈ Map P6 • Avda. Corrientes 1530 • 0800-333-5254

Bar La Paz
Opened in 1944, this café was once a favorite with the Avenue's theater crowd. Its interior is much changed, but it remains a decent enough hangout. ◈ Map P6 • Avda. Corrientes 1593 • 4373-3647

Cadore
The Cadore family started an ice-cream business in Italy in the 1880s and moved here in the 1950s. Flavors include homemade dulce de leche. ◈ Map P6 • Avda. Corrientes 1695 • 4373-9797

Teatro Gran Rex
The Gran Rex, built in 1937 in the Rationalist style, is one of the city's most iconic music and theater venues. Various international artists have played here. ◈ Map Q6 • Avda. Corrientes 857 • 4322-8000

Correo Central
Built in 1928 to house the central post office, Correo Central is an outstanding example of Beaux Arts architecture. ◈ Map R6 • Sarmiento 151

Left **Notorious** Center **La Biela** Right **Clásica y Moderna**

TOP 10 Bars and Cafés

1 El Banderín
This jewel of a café opened in 1926. Come for old-style charm, tasty sandwiches, and wine by the *copa*. ✪ *Map L5 • Guardia Vieja 3601, Almagro • 4862-7757*

2 Bar Celta
A relaxing escape with a lounge room and comfy sofas, Bar Celta is open 24 hours – a good choice for post-clubbing breakfasts. Live jazz plays on Wednesdays. ✪ *Map N6 • Sarmiento 1702, Congreso • 4371-7338*

3 The Shamrock
This bar attracts a stylish crowd. Its basement club fills on weekends when DJs spin house music. ✪ *Map N5 • Rodríguez Peña 1220, Recoleta • 4812-5332*

4 Milión
Set in a century-old mansion, this romantic bar-gallery features Art Nouveau staircases and stained-glass windows. ✪ *Map P5 • Paraná 1048, Recoleta • 4815-9925*

5 Notorious
At this jazz bar-café, musicians play in the back bar. In the front salon, you can slip on headphones and enjoy Coltrane or Ellington. ✪ *Map N5 • Avda. Callao 966, Barrio Norte • 4815-8473*

6 Jack The Ripper
This bar in an elegant belle époque mansion has chandeliers, antiques, and velvet sofas. ✪ *Map P4 • Libertad 1275, Recoleta • 4816-7508*

7 Clásica y Moderna
This sophisticated spot has bare-brick walls, low lighting, and a stone floor. Tango musicians play nightly. ✪ *Map N5 • Avda. Callao 892, Barrio Norte • 4812-8707*

8 Gran Bar Danzón
This Recoleta wine bar and restaurant has candlelit entrance stairs and an industrial-chic interior. The wine list is superb and the Modern Latin American cuisine divine. ✪ *Map P5 • Libertad 1161, Recoleta • 4811-1108*

9 Buller Brewing Company
This American-style bar produces its own beers. It fills up on weekends with a party crowd. ✪ *Map P4 • Presidente Roberto M. Ortíz 1827, Recoleta • 4808-9061*

10 La Biela
A historic corner café which was once a favorite haunt of the city's intelligentsia and Formula One racing driver Juan Manuel Fangio. The beautifully preserved interior opens onto an outside terrace. ✪ *Map P4 • Avda. Quintana 596, Recoleta • 4804-0449*

Price Categories

For a three-course meal for one with half a bottle of wine (or equivalent meal), taxes, and extra charges.

$	under US$10
$$	US$11–15
$$$	US$16–25
$$$$	US$26–35
$$$$$	over US$35

Interior of the Duhau Restaurant

🔟 Restaurants

1 Casa Salt Shaker
Try this supper club in the private home of chef Dan Perlman who whips up eclectic dishes. ◎ Map N4 • Uriburu (address supplied after booking) • Open 9pm–midnight Thu–Sat • www.casasaltshaker.com • $$$$$

2 Duhau Restaurant
Sample Gallic-inspired cuisine amid vaulted ceilings and sumptuous furnishings. ◎ Map P4 • Park Hyatt Buenos Aires, Avda. Alvear 1661 • 5171-1340 • $$$$

3 Nectarine 2.0
French cuisine is superbly prepared here. The wine list is outstanding and the ambience inviting. ◎ Map P4 • Vicente López 1661, Recoleta • 4813-6993 • $$$$

4 La Bourgogne
A superb wine list complements well-executed French cuisine in a stunning setting. ◎ Map P4 • Alvear Palace Hotel, Ayacucho 2023, Recoleta • 4805-3857 • $$$$

5 Cantina Pierino
Opened in 1909, this Italian cantina became the haunt of Astor Piazzolla and Aníbal Troilo (see p28). Home-made pastas are served along with meat and fish dishes. ◎ Map L5 • Lavalle 3499, Abasto • 4864-5715 • $$$$$

6 Status
Come to Status for delicious, authentic Peruvian cuisine at cheap prices. Try the lamb stew, superlative ceviche, and pisco sour. ◎ Map D1 • Virrey Cevallos 178, Congreso • 4382-8531 • $$

7 Campo dei Fiori
This Italian restaurant within a mansion house serves pastas, fish, and meats prepared in an open kitchen. ◎ Map D2 • Venezuela 1411, Montserrat • 4381-1800 • $

8 Cumaná
Regional specialties including locro and empanadas (see p53) are served at Cumaná, along with Italian dishes. ◎ Map N5 • Rodríguez Peña 1149, Recoleta • 4813-9207 • $

9 Restó
Set in a beautiful building, Restó serves exquisite Modern Argentinian cuisine. ◎ Map P5 • Montevideo 938, Recoleta • 4816-6711 • $$$$$

10 El Cuartito
Opened in 1934, El Cuartito is a classic family-run pizza joint. The Italian-style pizzas here are delicious. ◎ Map P5 • Talcahuano 937, Barrio Norte • 4816-1758 • $$$$

Left **Filete signs, Plaza Dorrego, San Telmo** Right **Parque Lezama**

San Telmo & La Boca

THE ROMANTIC BARRIOS OF SAN TELMO AND LA BOCA *are Buenos Aires'*
mythical old south. Once the heart of colonial Buenos Aires, San Telmo
beguiles with cobblestone streets of crumbling churches, colonial façades,
and dusty antiques stores. A working-class stronghold and magnet for
Bohemian artists, it remains, despite ongoing gentrification, a quarter of old

cafés, peeling stucco, and
tango bars. Tango emerged
from La Boca's conventillos
(tenement houses). La Boca
was the city's first port and
an African slave colony
before Italian immigrants
settled here in the 1880s.
One of the city's poorest
neighborhoods, it retains a
thriving cultural scene.

Art for sale on El Caminito

🔟 Sights

1. El Caminito
2. La Bombonera
3. Fundación Proa
4. Casa Mínima
5. Parque Lezama/ Museo Histórico Nacional
6. Plaza Dorrego
7. Museo de la Pasión Boquense
8. Iglesia Ortodoxa Rusa
9. Puente Trasbordador
10. El Zanjón

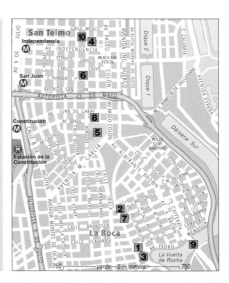

1 El Caminito

This curving, cobblestone street is famous for its colorful *conventillos* built by Italian immigrants. Made of corrugated zinc, the multi-hued paint scheme dates back to the original inhabitants, who coated the houses in leftover paint from the adjacent port. Today, the street is part of a vibrant scene that includes artists selling their wares, along with atmospheric tango bars and cafés. ◎ *Map G6*

2 La Bombonera

La Bombonera (The Chocolate Box) is the iconic home of Boca Juniors, the country's fanatically followed soccer club and Diego Maradona's beloved team. Built in 1940, the stadium is electrifying on game days. Its three distinct tiers rise almost vertically above the field. Bands also perform here. ◎ *Map G6*
• *Brandsen 805, La Boca • 4362-1100*
• *Open 10am–6pm daily • Adm*
• *www.bocajuniors.com.ar*

3 Fundación Proa

Housed in a recycled port building, the Fundación Proa is one of the city's most stimulating art spaces. Showcasing

The narrow façade of Casa Mínima

major art movements of the 20th century, the museum holds six temporary exhibitions each year. Previous memorable shows have included Diego Rivera and Marcel Duchamp. ◎ *Map G6 • Avda. Pedro de Mendoza 1929, La Boca • 4104-1000 • Open 11am–7pm Tue–Sun • Adm • www.proa.org*

4 Casa Mínima

The littlest house in San Telmo, Casa Mínima measures a tiny 8 ft by 26 ft (2 m by 8 m). It was originally a carriage entrance to the mansion next door, but was gifted by the owner to his freed slaves in 1813. ◎ *Map F3 • Pasaje Lorenzo 380, San Telmo • 4361-3002 • Tours: 10:30am, 3pm Mon–Fri • Adm*

The tiered seating at La Bombonera soccer stadium

San Telmo is the best place to buy filete, *a flamboyant folk art that commonly adorns storefronts, buses, and tango halls.*

Yellow Fever

In 1871 a deadly yellow fever outbreak engulfed Buenos Aires, devastating San Telmo. Richer inhabitants moved north to the new districts of Recoleta and Barrio Norte, initiating a period of decay in the city's south. The poverty gap between the city's wealthy northern neighborhoods and their poorer southern counterparts was thus born.

Parque Lezama/Museo Histórico Nacional

Popular with picnicking families, this landscaped park of tropical *tipa* trees, sweeping green spaces, and a broad viewing balcony, was once the private garden of the Lezama family. The Lezama home, a beautiful Italianate mansion, now houses the Museo Histórico Nacional – Argentina's national history museum. Fascinating displays recount Argentina's history from pre-Columbian times to the 20th century, and include the founding of Buenos Aires at this spot *(see p32)*. ◈ Map F4
• Defensa 1600, San Telmo • 4307-1182
• Open 11am–6pm daily • Adm

Plaza Dorrego

At the heart of San Telmo, lovely Plaza Dorrego is one of the city's oldest, most picturesque squares, ringed by old tango bars and cafés. Its origins go back to the 18th century, when gauchos came in by wagon to sell wares here. Today, it is famous for its bustling Sunday antiques and handicrafts market *(see p18)*. On weekdays, it is an ideal spot for alfresco drinks and snacks. ◈ Map F3

Museo de la Pasión Boquense

This chintzy museum revels in the glory of the Boca Juniors Club. Items on display include soccer trophies won over the years, vintage strips, and retro videos, including grainy 1920s footage. Expect gimmicky stuff too – have your "photo" taken with a grinning Maradona or buy a bottle of La Boca wine in the club store. ◈ Map G6 • Brandsen 805, La Boca • 4362-1100 • Open 10am–6pm daily • Adm • www.museoboquense.com

Iglesia Ortodoxa Rusa

The 1901 construction of this beautiful Russian Orthodox Church confirmed San Telmo as a bubbling melting pot of immigrant cultures. Its striking design – a blue-and-white onion-domed affair – was drawn up in Moscow and financed by Russia's imperial house along with members of Buenos Aires' Orthodox community. It mirrors exactly the churches of the Russian capital. ◈ Map F4 • Avda. Brasil 315, San Telmo

Puente Transbordador

La Boca's most iconic landmark, this magnificent transporter bridge is one of only a dozen or so of its kind left in the world. Built in 1908, its powerful iron frame straddles the polluted waters

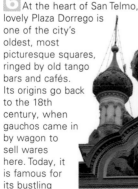

Iglesia Ortodoxa Rusa

Puente Transbordador

of Río Riachuelo, the river that separates the Buenos Aires metropolis from Gran Buenos Aires, the poverty and crime-ridden belt that rings the city's limits. Designed to transport pedestrians, cars, and trams across the river, it was replaced in 1939 by the Puente Nicolás Avellaneda, which now stands directly behind it. The bridge has appeared in numerous tango-themed films as an evocative icon. ⊕ *Map H6 • Pedro de Mendoza, cnr. Almirante Brown*

10 El Zanjón

El Zanjón (meaning "creek" in Spanish) is a 19th-century mansion and archeological jewel. The house was built in the 1840s for the Miguens family and later converted into a *conventillo* (tenement house), but it is what lies beneath it that is special. The building's foundations conceal the ruins of colonial houses, built by early settlers on the banks of two creeks that once converged at this spot. Tunnels built in the 19th century to cover the creeks for hygiene reasons run alongside the ruins. The site can be explored on stylized and fascinating tours. ⊕ *Map F3*
• *Defensa 755, San Telmo • 4361-3002*
• *Tours (1 hr tour, reservations only): 11am–3pm Mon–Fri, 1–6pm Sun*
• *Adm • www.elzanjon.com.ar*

A Day in San Telmo and La Boca

Morning

🕐 Start your day with a strong coffee at San Telmo's **Bar Plaza Dorrego** *(see p77)*. Stroll north on Dorrego, wandering in and out of antiques stores and art galleries as you go, and stopping at the **Mercado de San Telmo** *(see p19)* to buy fresh fruit. Then explore the subterranean tunnels and ruins at **El Zanjón** before resurfacing to visit **Casa Mínima** *(see p73)*. Head one block east and turn right. You are now on Balcarce. Soak in this street's colonial façades as you wander back to **Plaza Dorrego** and then onto **Parque Lezama**, visiting the **Iglesia Nuestra Señora de Belén** *(see p19)* en route. At Parque Lezama, enjoy a steak lunch at **Lezama** *(see p77)*, followed by a stroll of this lovely park.

Afternoon

Taking the No.29 bus from San Telmo, hop off at the end of the line in La Boca. Glance north and see the **Puente Transbordador**; a tango twirl south is **El Caminito** *(see p73)*. Explore this open-air museum, drinking in the colorful houses and browsing the artists' wares before turning right on Garibaldi. Walk three blocks to **La Bombonera** *(see p73)*. Take a stadium tour, stop by the **Museo de la Pasión Boquense**, and then head back the way you came. Back at the port, gorge on modern art at **Fundación Proa** *(see p73)* before returning to San Telmo. End your day with dinner and tango at **Patagonia Sur** *(see p77)*.

Avoid wandering around the foot of the Puente Transbordador – it is a crime hot spot.

Left **L'Ago** Center **Flavio Seratti Arte y Antigüedades** Right **Silvia Petroccia**

TOP 10 Galleries and Antique Stores

1 Gil Antigüedades
Collections include 1920s ladies' wear, antique purses, and 19th-century baby garments.
Map F3 • Humberto 1°, 412 • 4361-5019 • www.gilantiguedades.com.ar

2 Guevara Art Gallery
This gallery sells antique Art Deco and Art Nouveau furniture and other pieces. Map F3
• Defensa 982 • 4362-7718
• www.guevaragallery.com

3 Silvia Petroccia
This wonderful store is crammed with 18th- and 19th-century antiques from Italy and France. Map F3 • Defensa 1002
• 4362-0156 • www.spantiques.com.ar

4 Cualquier Verdura
The kitschest store in the area. Pick up an antique cheese grater or a Philippe Starck juicer.
Map F3 • Humberto Primero 517 • 4300-2474 • www.cualquierverdura.com.ar

5 HB Antigüedades
HB deals in furniture, paintings, and ornaments from 19th-century France. Map F3 • Defensa 1016 • 4362-7586 • www.hbantiques.com.ar

6 Espacio Ecléctico
This thriving gallery at the heart of San Telmo promotes emerging visual and plastic artists. The collections include sculpture, painting and photography. Map F4
• Humberto Primo 730 • 4307-1966
• www.espacioeclectico.com.ar

7 L'Ago
Modern interior design and decoration specialist L'Ago embraces the unconventional. Items are quirky and colorful, from garish pink sofa cushions to bracelets embellished with Catholic icons. Map F3 • Bolivak 644 • 4342-6148 • www.lagosantelmo.com

8 Jardín Oculto
This contemporary art gallery focuses on emerging artists' work. Map E2
• Venezuela 926 • 4343-0179
• www.jardinocultogaleria.com

9 Flavio Seratti Arte y Antigüedades
This store stocks antiques from the 1920s to 60s, including Art Deco pieces imported from Europe. Myriad curiosities include shark-skin jewelry boxes.
Map F3 • Defensa 914 • 4361-1258

10 Masottatorres
Specializing in Argentinian contemporary art and photography, this gallery focuses on avant-garde and tabooless themes.
Map F2 • Mexico 459
• 4331-6078 • www.masottatorres.com.ar

Around Town – San Telmo & La Boca

Price Categories

For a three-course meal for one with half a bottle of wine (or equivalent meal), taxes, and extra charges.

$	under US$10
$$	US$11–15
$$$	US$16–25
$$$$	US$26–35
$$$$$	over US$35

Wines on display at Brasserie Petanque

🔟 Bars and Restaurants

1 Aldo's Vinoteca
The food served at Aldo's is modern Argentinian, and there's a sommelier on hand to help you choose the perfect wine accompaniment. ✪ Map F2 • Moreno 372 • 5291-2380 • $$$

2 Bar Plaza Dorrego
Everything is atmospheric in San Telmo's most romantic watering hole, from the mosaic floor to the wooden wall cabinets and battered bar. ✪ Map F3 • Defensa 1098 • 4361-0141 • $$$

3 Gibraltar
This British-style pub is the best place in town for a pint. The food is great, with hot curries and huge burgers. There is also a pool table and a patio. ✪ Map F3 • Perú 895 • 4362-5310 • $$

4 Lezama
Author Ernesto Sábato penned *On Heroes and Tombs* at this classic family-run *parrilla*. The window tables overlook Parque Lezama *(see p74)*. ✪ Map F4 • Brasil 359 • 4361-0114 • $$$

5 Comedor Nikkai
The antidote to trendy sushi bars, Nikkai offers traditional Japanese cuisine. It is a favorite with the local Japanese community. ✪ Map F3 • Avda. Independencia 732 • 4300-5848 • $$$$$

6 Patagonia Sur
Owned by super-chef Francis Mallmann, this restaurant is a class apart. It has a wonderful decor and the food is traditional Argentinian. ✪ Map G6 • Rocha 801 • 4303 5917 • $$$$$

7 Brasserie Petanque
At this French-owned brasserie, the cuisine is straight off a Paris boulevard, the ambience is fabulous, and the menu is painted onto antique mirrors. ✪ Map F2 • Defensa 596 • 4342-7930 • $$$$$

8 Amici Miei
Enjoy great views over Plaza Dorrego *(see p74)*, while dining at Amici Miei. The menu features tasty Italian dishes. ✪ Map F3 • Defensa 1072 • 4361-2929 • $$$$$

9 Antigua Tasca de Cuchilleros
This *parrilla* is set in a restored 1730s house. Think thick adobe walls, original roof beams, and secret tunnels running under the floorboards. ✪ Map F3 • Carlos Calvo 319 • 4300-5798 • $$$$

10 Don Carlos
For a scrumptious and diverse dining experience head here, where *picadas* (tapas) of pizza, pasta, *pescado* (fish) and meat are plentiful. ✪ Map G6 • Brandsen 699 • 4362-2433 • $$$

Left **Plaza de Mayo** Right **Plaza San Martín**

Microcentro, Puerto Madero & Retiro

PLAZA DE MAYO HAS BEEN A FIXTURE *of* porteño *civic and cultural life for centuries. Nearby Puerto Madero, on the other hand, was incorporated officially into the city's barrio network only in 2007. The two areas reflect porteños' reverence for the historic as well as their enthusiastic embrace of the modern. The Plaza crowns Microcentro, the capital's commercial and financial center. From here the pedestrian mall Calle Florida careens off in a colorful barrage of bookstores, boutiques, and street performers, before terminating at the stately Plaza San Martín – the steeply sloping anchor of the Retiro neighborhood. Across Alem Avenue is the still-grand English-built train station that shares the neighborhood's name, while just south are the restored redbrick mercantile buildings and gleaming business parks that comprise Buenos Aires' latest reinvention, Puerto Madero.*

El Obelisco

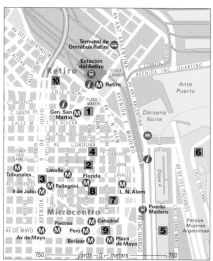

Sights

1. Plaza San Martín
2. Calle Florida
3. El Obelisco
4. Centro Cultural Borges
5. Puente de la Mujer
6. Reserva Ecológica Costanera Sur
7. Basílica Nuestra Señora de la Merced
8. Museo Mitre
9. Plaza de Mayo
10. Plaza Embajada de Israel

Preceding pages **Avenida de Mayo at dusk**

Plaza San Martín

The qualities of Buenos Aires' most carefully maintained plaza *(see p36)* are boundless. From its highest point at Avenida Santa Fe, a towering statue depicting triumphant General San Martín on horseback is set on a scalloped base – a popular lunch spot for the neighborhood's workers. Palms, majestic *lloronas*, and oaks shade those resting on the manicured grass. From late October till mid-December, purple jacaranda trees bloom along the stairway leading to the Falklands War memorial. ✎ *Map Q5*

Calle Florida

Ten blocks of unrelenting consumerism would be insufferable if not for Calle Florida's variety of shops and the quality of people-watching. Tiny snack kiosks sit alongside exquisite silver jewelers, young tango dancers and magicians gather crowds which, blithely entertained, impede pedestrian traffic, while sales clerks ply passersby with flyers for custom leather jackets. It is best to go with the flow from Plaza de Mayo toward Plaza San Martín as, by the 10th block, most appreciate the plaza's tranquility. ✎ *Map Q5*

El Obelisco

Monumental sculpture does not get much bolder than El Obelisco – a 220-ft (67-m) spire set on 9 de Julio. The 1936 structure was built to commemorate the 400th anniversary of Buenos Aires' founding, and it now serves as a point of orientation for visitors and porteños, as well as being the traditional place for football fans to congregate should their team win *(see p20)*.

Equestrian statue of San Martín

Centro Cultural Borges

However incongruous it may be to find a vital cultural center inside a shopping mall, the Centro Cultural Borges is an enveloping experience. The three-level space is dedicated to Argentina's grandest writer *(see p33)*, exhibiting Borges' letters, poems, and effects. It is also a performance space, where avant-garde tango shows draw passionate audiences. Its visual arts wing has held shows of Joan Miró and Salvador Dalí's work. ✎ *Map Q5 • Galerías Pacífico, Viamonte 525 • 5555-5359 • Open 10am–9pm Mon–Sat, noon–9pm Sun • Adm • www.ccborges.org.ar*

Centro Cultural Borges housed in Galerías Pacífico

Lunch – Microcentro Style

For people who take a sandwich back to the computer, the lunchtime customs of Microcentro's workers might inspire admiration and jealousy. Workers eat out at a restaurant or a shady patch of Plaza de Mayo. A coffee follows at Martínez or Havanna, and in good weather, a short nap under a palm. Two hours later, it is back to work.

5 Puente de la Mujer

When opened in December 2001, Spanish architect Sergio Calatrava's Puente de la Mujer, so called for the streets in Puerto Madero bearing names of famous Argentinian women, was intended to herald the city's entry into the 21st century. However, the government's collapse stole the bridge's headlines. Its striking form cannot be denied though, evoking a male dancer pressing into his female partner in clear, elegant homage to the tango. ◈ *Map G2 • Dique 3*

6 Reserva Ecológica Costanera Sur

A network of gravel paths wind through this stupendous eco-logical reserve. High marsh grasses, *ombú* trees, and flowering bushes play host to seabirds, lizards, and songbirds. Shaded picnic areas, popular on warm days, afford unimpeded river views. Check the website for guided moonlit tours. ◈ *Map H1 • Avda. Tristán Achával Rodríguez 1550 • 0800 444-5343 • Open Apr–Oct: 8am–6pm Tue–Sun; Nov–Mar: 8am–7pm Tue–Sun • www.buenosaires.gov.ar*

7 Basilica Nuestra Señora de la Merced

This 1779 basilica set amid Microcentro's bustle is the third Our Lady of Mercy on this site, the first dating back to 1604. Baroque and gilded, its altars are some of the city's finest. Also notable is its façade's politicized relief, depicting General Belgrano (1770–1820) offering victory trophies to the Señora, earned in battle against the Spanish. ◈ *Map F1 • Calle Reconquista 207 • Open 8am–7pm daily*

8 Museo Mitre

Opened as a museum in 1907, the former residence of mid-19th-century president Bartólome Mitre presents a detailed view of how he lived the semi-retired life amid Microcentro's madness. His formidable library and reading

The elegant Puente de la Mujer

Basílica Nuestra Señora de la Merced

room contains thick volumes as well as letters from Argentinian generals. Period furnishings, from original porcelain bath fixtures to the courtyard's Spanish tiles, are in excellent repair. 🗺 *Map F1 • Calle San Martín 336 • 4394-8240 • Open 1–5:30pm Mon–Fri; closed Jan–Feb • Adm*

9 Plaza de Mayo

The Plaza's symmetry belies the many upheavals that shaped its current dimensions. To make room for Avenida de Mayo, three arches were shorn off its arcade in 1889. In 1931, avenue Julio A. Rocha was completed, requiring the demolition of three more arches, leaving us with the view we have today *(see pp8–9)*.

10 Plaza Embajada de Israel

Twenty-nine trees planted for each of the murdered bear witness to the 1992 terrorist attack on Israel's Argentinian embassy *(see p33)*. The site is now a plaza, where the victims' names are etched into a wall. The embassy's former outline is still imprinted in the adjacent building, providing a sense of the tragedy's physical scale. 🗺 *Map Q4 • Cnr. Calles Suipacha and Arroyo • Open daily • Adm free*

A Day Around Microcentro, Puerto Madero, and Retiro

Morning

🕐 From the intersection of Avenida de Mayo and Avenida 9 de Julio, (serviced by Líneas A or C) get a glimpse of **El Obelisco** *(see p20)* monument from Don Quixote's vantage. Walk along de Mayo toward **Plaza de Mayo**, taking in the **El Cabildo** *(see p8)* and paying respects to the Grand Liberator San Martín inside **La Catedral Metropolitana** *(see p8)*. Continue down Calle San Martín for a late-morning coffee and *alfajor* *(see p53)* inside one of **Galería Güemes'** *(see p39)* cafés, and bask in the passageway's early 20th-century grandeur. Exit onto **Calle Florida** *(see p81)* for a block of rampant consumerism before turning onto J.D. Perón and following it all the way to Puerto Madero.

Afternoon

Grab a water bottle at a Puerto Madero kiosk, hail a radio taxi bound for the **Reserva Ecológica Costanera Sur's** northern entrance, and keep eyes sharp inside the park for coastal birdlife. Rest for a while at a shaded picnic spot and take in the river and the city's skyline view. Afterward, trace your steps back to Avenida Córdoba and follow it up to Calle San Martín for well-deserved, creative pizzas at **FILO** *(see p85)*. From there, head towards Retiro to indulge in retail therapy amid the artisan shops *(see pp38–9)*, before resting under the trees at the verdant **Plaza San Martín** *(see p81)*.

Left **Plata Nativa** Right **Millai Sumaj**

🔟 Stores

Plata Nativa
South American folk art and jewelry are showcased in this evocative space. 🗺 Map Q5
• Galería del Sol, Calle Florida 860
• 4312-1398

Blaqué
This swish store stocks glam leather jackets, handbags, and shoes worthy of a Fendi store. 🗺 Map Q5 • Galerías Pacífico, Calle Florida 725 • 5555-5215

Antigüedades Antigüa
Vintage Argentinian toys, books, and housewares are available here. 🗺 Map Q6 • Calle Suipacha 228 • 5029-0133

Polo Club
Well-crafted cotton casual wear and quality leather accessories lend a country-club aesthetic to this small space. 🗺 Map R6
• Calle Juana Manuela Gorriti 740, Dique 4 • 4331-0705

Adolfo Martínez Armas Antiguas
This longtime Galerías Larreta tenant sells national and international military memorabilia. 🗺 Map Q5 • Calle Florida 971
• 4311-7305

Millai Sumaj
Smart, contemporary women's fashions are hand-crafted from Patagonian and llama wool at Millai Sumaj. Raw materials are purchased from indigenous people within Argentina. 🗺 Map Q5 • Galerías Larreta, Calle Florida 971

Artistas Jóvenes Argentinos
This is possibly the best place to purchase the work of some of Argentina's most progressive young painters. 🗺 Map Q5 • Galerías Larreta, Calle Florida 971 • 4893-3666

Autoria
Housewares, limited-run silkscreened T-shirts, art books, and mixed-media pieces, all by local artists, give Autoria a touch of MALBA (see pp22–3). 🗺 Map Q5 • Calle Suipacha 1025 • 5252-2474

Se Dice de Mí
1960s-cinema inspired tees, handbags fashioned from recycled materials, and lingerie fill this spacious shop. 🗺 Map Q5
• Calle Maipú 944 • 4311-1005

Tango Brujo
Numerous couples have been set twirling in the Nouveau Tango style by Tango Brujo. Its handsome ground-level shop stocks delicate tango fashions, an excellent music selection, and top-quality footwear, with expert fittings. 🗺 Map E3 • Calle Independencia 1099
• 4325-8264

Price Categories

For a three-course		
meal for one with half	**$**	under US$10
a bottle of wine (or	**$$**	US$11–15
equivalent meal), taxes,	**$$$**	US$16–25
and extra charges.	**$$$$**	US$26–35
	$$$$$	over US$35

Florida Garden

🔟 Bars and Restaurants

1 La Cigale
Dark electronica and bossa nova sounds waft through this moody bar, popular with artists and poets. ✪ Map Q5 • Avda. 25 de Mayo 597 • 4893-2332 • $

2 Cabaña Las Lilas
The shock of splurging at arguably the city's best steakhouse can be tempered at lunchtime when beef prices are slightly more budget-friendly.
✪ Map R6 • Alicia Moreau de Justo 516, Puerto Madero • 4313-1336 • $$$$$

3 Bengal
Make sure you reserve in advance to sample the fascinating fusion of Indian and Italian dishes here. ✪ Map Q5 • Arenales 837 • 4314-2926 • $$$$$

4 FILO
The fanciful decor reflects the creativity of this pizzeria with signature pies outnumbered only by the salad combos. FILO also rotates painting exhibitions through its space. ✪ Map Q5 • Calle San Martín 975 • 4311-1871 • $$$

5 Dill & Drinks
Order a herby cocktail at the bar first, then move on to the bistro-style menu in the cozy restaurant. The atmosphere is fun and friendly.
✪ Map Q5 • San Marín 986, Microcentro • 4515-0675 • $$$$

6 Tomo 1
Delicate porteño cuisine is served in a dignified room here. ✪ Map P6 • Calle Carlos Pellegrini 521, Microcentro • 4326-6695 • $$$$$

7 El Patio
This bustling and affordable place serves humbly prepared porteño fare. ✪ Map Q6 • Ex-Convento Grande de San Ramón Nonato, Calle Reconquista 269 • 4343-0290 • $

8 Dadá
Amid bright furnishings and antique fixtures, business types and nattily dressed scenesters share lunches or an extend happy hour. ✪ Map Q5 • Calle San Martín 941 • 4314-4787 • $$$

9 Florida Garden
The modern look obscures Florida Garden's past life as an intellectuals' haven. Borges (see p59) and his cadre held debates over pizzas here. ✪ Map Q5 • Calle Florida 899 • 4312-7902 • $

10 Sipan
This hidden-away Peruvian and Japanese fusion restaurant serves exquisite rice and fish dishes. Try their ocean-fresh ceviche, a local favorite, or the tiradito, a Japanese version. There's an outside patio with heaters in winter.
✪ Map Q5 • Paraguay 624 • 4311-6875 • $$$$$

Left **Plaza Serrano** Right **A chic boutique on a street in Palermo**

Palermo

PALERMO IS THE CURRENT INTERNATIONAL *buzzword for all things edgy and fashionable about Argentina – deservedly so, given the profusion of couture boutiques, minimalist hotels, and swish restaurants that have sprung up in the* barrio, *post-economic crisis. The tattoos and asymmetrical haircuts on display in the renovated* casas chorizos *of Palermo Viejo, though, would cause a scandal amid the Neo-Classical embassies and handsome mansions of Palermo Chico. Between them, however, is plenty of common ground: acres of Buenos Aires' finest parkland, a swath of green extending from Recoleta through the barrio of Belgrano.*

Gallery displaying contemporary art at MALBA

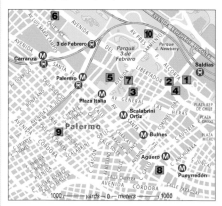

TOP10 Sights

1. MALBA
2. Jardín Japonés
3. Museo Evita
4. Museo de Arte Popular José Hernández
5. La Rural
6. Campo Argentino de Polo
7. Jardín Zoológico
8. Museo Xul Solar
9. Plaza Serrano
10. Planetario Galileo Galilei

MALBA

1 Until recently, Latin American art was not considered highly collectible by the commercial art industry. In the 1980s and 90s, however, Eduardo Constantini's aggressive acquisition of *rioplatense* art started a worldwide re-examination of Xul Solar, Hélio Oitica, Roberto Matta, and others, making their auction prices reach record highs. His prizes now decorate the world-class art museum MALBA *(see pp22–3).*

Jardín Japonés

2 The images of koi ponds and bridges in the tourist brochures belong to the Jardín Japonés, a Japanese garden with bonsai trees, festive shrines, and pagodas. The garden, a gift from the city's Japanese community, also contains an excellent sushi café that serves impeccably fresh sashimi. ◎ *Map M2*
• *Casares 2966* • *4804-4922* • *Open 10am–6pm daily; restaurant: 10am–6pm, 7:30pm–midnight Wed–Mon* • *Adm*
• *www.jardinjapones.org.ar*

Jardín Japonés

Museo Evita

Museo Evita

3 For a woman whose public-speaking bombast and charisma rivaled her borderline-fascist husband's, Eva Perón is remembered for her grace, beauty, and delicate health. Museo Evita, an elegant building, was formerly a lodge for Argentinian women who moved to Buenos Aires to find work, dedicated by Evita in 1948. The ex-First Lady's dresses, letters, and identity cards share space with propaganda posters and subtitled video clips captured at political rallies. ◎ *Map L3* • *Calle Lafinur 2988*
• *4807-9433* • *Open 11am–7pm Tue–Sun*
• *Adm* • *Free English-language tours available* • *www.museoevita.org*

Museo de Arte Popular José Hernández

4 No other museum evokes the grand, diverse country surrounding the capital like this one, named in honor of Argentina's own Homer, José Hernández *(see p33)*, author of the 1872 folkloric epic poem *Martín Fierro*. Two levels of folk crafts, textiles, weaponry, and jewelry, produced from icy Tierra del Fuego to the sub-Amazonian jungles of Misiones, are assembled around a flowering garden inside this petite former hotel. ◎ *Map M2* • *Avda. del Libertador 2373*
• *4803-2384* • *Open 1–7pm Wed–Fri, 10am–8pm Sat, Sun* • *Adm* • *Guided tour: 4801-9019* • *www.museohernandez.org.ar*

Palermo Not-So-Viejo

Few would have predicted that a neighborhood known for auto mechanics and homes for the aged would lead Buenos Aires' post-crisis boom. Palermo Viejo's Italianate *casas chorizos* were renovated to house the boutiques and restaurants that dominate its streets today. It is also called Palermo Soho as a nod to its new tenants' urban-chic sensibilities.

La Rural

The Sociedad Argentina Predio la Rural, or La Rural, has occupied a hallowed position during its 120-plus years at the corner of Sarmiento and Santa Fe. Equestrian shows, livestock auctions, the annual agricultural fair *(see p42)*, and other exhibitions such as BA Fashion Week and Arte BA take place here. ✪ Map L2 • Avda. Sarmiento 2704 • 4777-5500 • www.larural.com.ar

Campo Argentino de Polo

Polo, the aristocratic bastion of sportsmanship and breeding, has been popular in Argentina for over a century now. Palermo's Neo-Classical Campo Argentino de Polo, also known as La Catedral, holds 30,000 spectators and is the spiritual heart of the sport in Argentina. Tickets for December's Open tournament can be difficult to come by, but the spring season's qualifying matches serve as great entree to the experience, and come at cheaper prices. ✪ Map K1 • Arevalo 3065 • 4777-6444 • Open Sep–Dec • www.aapolo.com; www.ticketek.com.ar

Jardín Zoológico

Many of the animals' dwellings in this zoo emulate their native settings – Indian elephants roam around a miniature temple, while red pandas mill about a Chinese pavilion. Most famous here are the white Bengal tigers. ✪ Map L2 • Cnr Avda. Las Heras & Sarmiento • 4011-9900 • Open 10am–6pm Tue–Sun • Adm • www.zoobuenosaires.com.ar

Elephants at Jardín Zoológico

Museo Xul Solar

The boundless imagination of Argentina's greatest abstract Expressionist is just barely contained within this museum that once served as the artist's home.

Campo Argentino de Polo

Drago (Dragon), Museo Xul Solar

The permanent exhibition documents Solar's figurative water colors, owing a debt to European influences and development of his metaphysical language. The multi-level gallery allows Solar's color palette, all luminous pastels, to stand out *(see p22)*. ⊗ *Map M4 • Calle Laprida 1212 • 4824-3302 • Open noon–8pm Tue–Fri, noon–7pm Sat • Adm • Tours 4pm Tue, Thu; 3:30pm Sat • www.xulsolar.org.ar*

Plaza Serrano
Plaza Serrano, also known as Plazoleta Cortázar, has evolved into the heart of the Palermo Viejo/Soho/Hollywood nexus. From this rather ordinary plaza, Palermo Viejo's most fashionable streets shoot off in every direction. ⊗ *Map K3*
• Cnr Calles Borges & Honduras

Planetario Galileo Galilei
With a huge sphere poised on three legs and looking like a science-fiction movie's alien transport, this planetarium is one of the continent's top astronomical research facilities. Its shows contain imagery from satellite missions. The greatest attraction are the three prehistoric meteorites recovered from the northwest provinces. ⊗ *Map M1 • Cnr Avda. Sarmiento and Belisa Vío Roldán • 4771-6629 • Shows (one per hour): 1–4:30pm Tue–Fri, 2–6pm Sat, Sun & holidays • Adm • www.planetario.gov.ar*

An Afternoon of Palermo Flair

Afternoon

Start your afternoon wending through the labyrinthine streets east of Avenida Figueroa Alcorta, past Buenos Aires' fine mansions and embassies, and up to **MALBA** *(see p87)*. Then, debate whether the pan-Latin American masterworks at MALBA are or are not overshadowed by the striking building itself. Make sure not to skip the fabulous gift shop. Afterward, continue up Avenida Figueroa Alcorta to the **Jardín Japonés** *(see p87)*. Should the monstrous koi fish in its central pond arouse your sushi appetite, get some *omakase* (or if not, delicious cakes and tea) at the garden's restaurant. Next, glimpse the life of Argentina's first lady, Evita, at **Museo Evita** *(see p87)* on Calle Lafinur.

Evening

Continuing up to Plaza Italia, hop on a 93 bus and get out around Calle Honduras, the main drag through Palermo Hollywood's international bistros. To share a *picada* and some happy-hour beers, turn down Honduras and right before Calle Bonpland, and head inside **Acabar** *(see p92)* for a round of beers over Jenga or a boardgame. Given the gaudy, thrift-store decor, the depth of **Acabar**'s cocktail menu makes for a pleasant surprise. Later, have a look around the intersection of Honduras and Bonpland to get dinner ideas; **HG Restaurant**'s tasting menu is a great choice in the vicinity *(see p93)*.

Left **María Cher** Center **La Casa de las Botas** Right **Félix**

🔟 Neighborhood Stores

1 Carla Di Sí
Stylish spectacles and sunglasses from Latin America's only eyewear designer. 🟡 *Map K4* • *Gurruchaga 1677* • *4832-1655*

2 Hermanos Estebecorena
Functional menswear with a trendy twist is designed by two siblings who are industrial designers. There's a range of shoes and underwear too, making this a comprehensive shop to get kitted out. 🟡 *Map J2* • *El Salvador 5960* • *4772-2145*

3 La Casa de las Botas
Leather boots for all equestrian disciplines are available here. The shop's shorter styles, called Jodhpur boots, strike profiles for fashion runways. 🟡 *Map K2* • *Calle Paraguay 5062* • *4776-0762*

4 La Pasionaria
A riotous jumble of modernist and Deco furnishings, lamps, and curios are housed in this restored yet raw warehouse at the western fringe of Palermo Viejo. 🟡 *Map J3* • *Calle Godoy Cruz 1541* • *4773-0563*

5 María Cher
The inventory of María Cher's exquisite casual cottons and chic satins is kept in constant rotation. 🟡 *Map K4* • *Calle El Salvador 4724* • *4833-4736*

6 Sabater Hnos. Fábrica de Jabones
Hand soaps of every imaginable texture and color fill the bins and shelves of this festive shop, where the goods are made on the premises. 🟡 *Map K3* • *Calle Gurruchaga 1821* • *4833-3004*

7 Capital Diseño y Objetos
Capital carries leather table mats and modernist chairs along with children's furniture and toys. 🟡 *Map K4* • *Calle Honduras 4958* • *4834-6555*

8 Félix
With button-downs, perfectly cut jeans, and primary-color tees for men, Felix also has a Recoleta branch *(Libertad 1627)*. 🟡 *Map K3* • *Calle Guatemala 5200* • *4775-0380*

9 A.Y. Not Dead
For clubwear with a hand-made feel and edgier sensibility than that at Bond Street *(see p39)*, visit this shop. 🟡 *Map L4* • *Calle Gurruchaga 1637* • *4833-2999*

10 Humawaca
This is the place for edgy, attractive leather accessories, such as i-pad holders, laptop briefcases, and innovative handbags in quirky colours. There is also a range of wallets and gloves. 🟡 *Map K4* • *El Salvador 4692* • *4832-2262*

Left **República de Acá** Right **Pabellón 4**

🔟 Multispaces

Eterna Cadencia
This is that rare bookstore that makes one feel worldly. Eterna Cadencia stocks lovely art books and a selection of English titles, and has a cozy atrium café. It is also a publishing house. ◈ Map J3 • Calle Honduras 5574 • 4774-4100

Pabellón 4
In addition to its showcases of local industrial designers' works and performance art, Pabellón IV, a veteran multi-purpose arts spaces, also features a moody bar/café. ◈ Map J3 • Calle Uriarte 1332 • 4772-8745

Carnal
Famous for its terrace pre-parties, the trailer-trash decor of bar/lounge Carnal draws even reserved drinkers out of their shells. ◈ Map J3 • Calle Niceto Vega 5511 • 4772-7582

Oxiro
Set in a restored Palermo house, multimedia space Oxiro adds artistic grit with photography installations. ◈ Map J4 • Calle Gurruchaga 1358 • 4771-3563

Escarlata
A nexus of neighborhood artistry, openings here are boisterous. ◈ Map J4 • Calle Serrano 1408 • 4833-9373

República de Acá
Buenos Aires' golden age of comedy is paid homage at this nightlife mainstay. It is plastered with caricatures and film stills. ◈ Map J4 • Federico Lacrose 601 • 4581-0278

Arte de Mafia
After 10pm, jazz groups complement the Italian dishes here with live renditions of *canzonette italiane* and *tarantelle*. ◈ Map K3 • Calle El Salvador 4975 • 4831-9213

Brujas
Apart from a pizza menu to rival that of FILO *(see p85)*, Brujas boasts diverse canvases by neighborhood artists. ◈ Map K3 • Calle Costa Rica 4827 • 4832-7919

Spell Café
The spacious Spell Café comprises three levels of pizza/pasta-geared dining and beer drinking, an art gallery, and a performance space. ◈ Map K4 • Calle Malabia 1738 • 4832-3389

Pampa Picante
The handsome Pampa Picante betters its beef-centric competitors with *asado* (grill) lessons, in groups of two to six. Graduates of the lesson eat what they cook. ◈ Map K4 • Calle Nicaragua 4610 • 4833-7251

Left **Mundo Bizarro** Right **Acabar**

🔟 Bars

1 Bar 6
Despite its cool minimalism, Bar 6 manages to be a relaxed spot for carefully prepared drinks and snacks. ✪ Map K4 • Calle Armenia 1676 • 4833-6807

2 Acabar
The area's pioneer, Acabar's staying power is additionally rooted in liberal measures and guilt-inducing bar grub. ✪ Map J3 • Calle Honduras 5733 • 4772-0845

3 Mundo Bizarro
Low-art hallmarks make Mundo Bizarro a slice of Southern California kitsch. The tattooed barmen know their way around whiskey cocktails too. ✪ Map J4 • Calle Serrano 1222 • 4773-1967

4 Soul Café
The DJ spins Motown, jazz, and hip-hop at one of the first resto-bars in the Las Cañitas neighborhood. The sushi here is good too. ✪ Map K1 • Calle Baez 246 • 4778-3115

5 Sugar
This popular ex-pat haunt has excellent-value happy hours every evening and decent American-style bar food, such as burgers and chicken wings. It is renowned for 1980s and 1990s music. ✪ Map K3 • Calle Costa Rica 4619 • 4831-3276

6 Crónico Bar
The façade here opens onto the street, promising a raucous good time. ✪ Map K3 • Calle Jorge L. Borges 1646 • 4833-0708

7 Tiempo de Gitanos Bar y Fonda
Reserve in advance for the dinner shows at this riotously colored flamenco bar and restaurant. ✪ Map J3 • Calle El Salvador 5575 • 4776-6143

8 Frank's
Once you've figured out the password from Facebook or Twitter to get in, kick back with the cool crowd at this modern-day speakeasy. ✪ Map J2 • Arévalo 1445 • www.franks-bar.com

9 Magdalena's Party
A popular spot with a young crowd, Maggie's offers good drinks, with revelers often spilling out onto the street. ✪ Map K3 • Calle Thames 1795 • 4833-9127

10 878
Nobody arrives at 878 by accident, as it is detached from the Palermo Viejo bustle and located in adjacent Villa Crespo. The lounge fits about 50 cocktail sippers around its weathered tables. There is also a secret back bar. ✪ Map J4 • Calle Thames 878 • 4773-1098

Price Categories

For a three-course meal for one with half a bottle of wine (or equivalent meal), taxes, and extra charges.

$	under US$10
$$	US$11–15
$$$	US$16–25
$$$$	US$26–35
$$$$$	over US$35

HG Restaurant

TOP 10 Restaurants

1 Ølsen
The relatively light cuisine of Scandinavia has made a huge splash with meat-reared porteños, due almost entirely to Ølsen. Try the open-faced gravlax sandwiches. ◎ Map J3 • Calle Gorriti 5870 • 4776-7677 • $$$$$

2 La Cabrera
Reserve, or arrive early for Palermo's best meat, served in a cozy, classic street-corner bistro or under the sidewalk awning. ◎ Map J4 • Cabrera 5099 • 4831-7002 • $$$$$

3 Casa Cruz
Celebrities nibble *duck magret* and sip special-reserve wines at Casa Cruz. ◎ Map J3 • Calle Uriarte 1658 • 4833-1112 • $$$$$

4 El Trapiche
In this classic white-tablecloth *parrilla*, Malbecs accompany steak. The tenderloin is among Palermo's best, and the delicious ice-cream desserts are best shared. ◎ Map K2 • Calle Paraguay 5099 • 4772-7343 • $$$

5 El Preferido de Palermo
Dishes served in this 75-year-old Italian grocery include *tortilla Espanola* (Spanish omelet) with a side of sauerkraut. ◎ Map K3 • Jorge Luis Borges 2108 • 4774-6585 • $$$

6 Kensho
Organic vegetarian cuisine with an oriental flair makes a welcome change from meat-heavy menus. ◎ Map J2 • El Salvador 5783 • 4778-0655 • $$$

7 Paraje Arévalo
This charming corner eatery offers a delectable tasting menu, which can be paired with wine. The focus is on simplicity with a dash of molecular gastronomy. ◎ Map J2 • Arévalo 1502 • 4775-7759 • $$$$$

8 Azema Exotic Bistró
Choose from lamb masala, Vietnamese noodle dishes, tandoor-baked salmon, and appetizers listed on the eclectic menu. ◎ Map J3 • Calle Angel Carranza 1875 • 4774-4191 • $$$$

9 HG Restaurant
The Spanish-influenced dishes here are served tapas style. Indulge in a three-hour tasting menu. ◎ Map J2 • Soler 5862 • 3220-6800 • $$$$$

10 Bio
Inventive, all-organic, all-vegetarian fare that champions local ingredients is prepared here. The atmosphere is casual, with bright wood furnishings and massive windows. ◎ Map K2 • Calle Humboldt 2192 • 4774-3880 • $$$

Left **Punta del Este** Right **Tigre**

Beyond Buenos Aires

WHILE BUENOS AIRES *is the obvious focal point of the River Plate region, its surrounding communities – sprouting up from jungle-like river deltas or sprawling, rugged mountain terrain – kick with local rhythms of their own. Fruit and lumber have drifted downriver from the labyrinthine waterways of Tigre, just 16 miles (25 km) north of Retiro, for over a century. The romantic spirit of the boundless Pampa and the gauchos who tamed it is celebrated in*

the southwestern Mataderos and the historical, handsome village of San Antonio de Areco. With flights and ferries leaving for the walkable capital of Montevideo, the colonial jewel Colonia del Sacramento, and the fashionable beach destination Punta del Este, Uruguay figures in any discussion of favorite porteño get-aways. These destinations usually cater well to impulsive travelers.

Colonia del Sacramento

🔟 Sights

1. Montevideo
2. Colonia del Sacramento
3. Mar del Plata
4. Tandil
5. Tigre
6. San Antonio de Areco
7. Punta del Este
8. Pinamar
9. Mataderos
10. Isla Martín García

Some advance planning is recommended when visiting this region during holidays.

Plaza Independencia, Montevideo

Montevideo

Nearly half of Uruguay's 3.7 million citizens live in the capital of Montevideo. Legendary for their hospitality and civic pride, they congregate at all hours in Plaza Independencia *(see p98)* and tuck into the local grill specialty, *chivito* (a thin steak sandwich). Ciudad Vieja mirrors Buenos Aires' San Telmo in its reinvention as a nightlife and dining neighborhood. Unlike its massive River Plate neighbor, Montevideo feels like a coastal city with its municipal beaches and *paseos* overlooking the deep blue waters. ⊗ *Map B4*

Colonia del Sacramento

Fifty minutes from Puerto Madero on Buquebus' fastest vessels *(see p25)*, Colonia is an 18th-century town on a strategic outcrop of Uruguayan soil. Some choose to spend the night in one of its charming *posadas* or to rent scooters to explore surrounding beaches. What everyone invariably does is soak up the colonial atmosphere at a sidewalk café *(see pp24–5)*.

Mar del Plata

A virtual 1:20 scale model of Buenos Aires, Mar del Plata is located 5 hours from la Capital. Its cosmopolitan attractions and coastal high-rises are about excitement, not relaxation. Playa Bristol, the principal beach, teems with families under umbrellas and vendors hawking everything from popcorn to massages. Seafood, brought in by emblematic fleets of yellow-hulled fishing boats, features prominently on menus. ⊗ *Map B6*

Tandil

With the horizon-flat Pampa commencing just beyond Buenos Aires and extending for hundreds of miles, Tandil's rugged 1,640 ft (500 m) hills prove irresistible for *porteños* without time or pesos for Patagonia. El Centinela, a 23-ft (7-m) high rock balancing atop a hill, can be reached by a ski chairlift. In the town, plaza-side bars and delicatessens stocking locally produced jams, cheeses, and dry sausages provide ample reward for the returning day hikers. ⊗ *Map A5*

Upriver on the Railroad

The Tren de la Costa (US$5 round trip) runs between Bartólome Mitre and Tigre. Take a 30-minute ride from Retiro on the Mitre line to Bartólome Mitre. A pedestrian causeway connects to the train's base, Estación Maipú. Between Maipú and Tigre is San Isidro, a riverside parkland, and quaint stationhouses. The Tren de la Costa ticket lasts a full day.

Tigre

The region's shortest and most modern train, the Tren de la Costa (see also p60) terminates at Tigre, the former agricultural hub and porteño playground at the confluence of the Luján and Tigre rivers. Palatial rowing clubs and boathouses line Paseo Victorica, where teak-hulled boats offer excursions under the delta's willows and coniferous species. The port itself counts an amusement park, casino, and an artisans' market. Map B4

San Antonio de Areco

Just 68 miles (110 km) south-west of Buenos Aires, this unspoilt cowboy town boasts a historic center. Buildings from the 18th and 19th centuries and wrought-iron lamps line the cobblestone streets around Plaza Ruíz de Arellano. Just outside of town, family-owned estancias raise cattle and horses. San Antonio fills up for its annual Día de la Tradición in November. Map A4 • www.sanantoniodeareco.com

Punta del Este

Come summer, Buenos Aires' media turns breathless in its coverage of illustrious holiday-makers sunning, gambling, and clubbing in Punta del Este, Uruguay, the region's answer to Miami Beach. The celebrity scene, however, cannot compare to Punta's natural beauty – white sand dunes overlooked by rugged bluffs. Budget airline Sol makes the hour-long flight multiple times daily from Aeroparque Jorge Newbury during high season, and accommodations cover every price bracket. Map C4

Pinamar

Perched on a forested point, Pinamar is named for the incongruous pine groves planted by the resort town's founding family. For porteños, Pinamar is synonymous with golf, which has in turn brought more families into this previously posh beach

A boat trip down the scenic Tigre River

Typical gaucho and his horse

destination. In contrast to the pebble-strewn sands to its north and south, Pinamar's shores are soft and golden. ✎ *Map B5*

Mataderos

For visitors with no time to visit an *estancia* or San Antonio de Areco, the weekend gaucho fair in Mataderos is an excellent alternative. Its southwest neighborhood was once Buenos Aires' meat-packing hub, but today very few plants remain. Instead, a weekend folk fair has sprung up, with live *folclóre* music and dancing, displays of gaucho horse mastery, and *artesanía*. ✎ *Map A4 • Calle Lisandro de la Torre & Avda. Directorio • Fair: Apr–mid-Dec: 11am–9pm Sun; late Jan–Mar: 1–9pm Sat • www.feriademataderos.com.ar*

Isla Martín García

The thick vegetation on this small delta island gives the impression of an impenetrable citadel. Interestingly, political prisoners were lodged here until the 1960s. Today, the abandoned prison and the landscape attract porteño daytrippers and savvy foreigners. At Christmas time, the island's sole bakery works overtime producing fruit-cake similar to *panettone* (a sweet bread from Milan). ✎ *Map A4*

A Day in Montevideo

Morning

Pack a beach bag and head for a typical breakfast of *tostadas* and coffee at one of the excellent cafés there. City buses leave from Avenida 18 de Julio, the main thoroughfare at the plaza, to **Playa Ramírez**, 1 mile (2 km) east. Set right in front of **Montevideo's** *(see p95)* leafy, landscaped **Parque Rodo**, the beach is favored for its cleanliness, proximity to Ciudad Vieja, and its irresistable mix of grandeur (the Neo-Colonial Mercosur regional trade-block offices form its backdrop) and honky tonk. A few amusement park rides and *chivito* stands nearby keep kids happy and fed too. For some shade, cross the Rambla to **Parque Rodo** and rent a bike or paddle boat from one of the numerous outfitters.

Evening

The streets of Ciudad Vieja, especially the Calle Sarandí, form a nexus of dining and drinking. Share an inexpensive bottle of the local varietal, *tannat*, at **Baar Fun Fun** *(see p99)*, and ask your bartender for his favorite restaurant in the zone. A solid choice is **El Callejón**, a tiny resto-pub with excellent antipasti, fish, plus live acoustic guitar (Calle Bartólome Mitre 1386, $$). Nightclubs begin to pump around midnight, with the crowd descending on **KEY** (Calle 25 de Mayo 745) which, despite its commercial name, deploys a plush lounge, bar, and dancefloor over three levels of a converted 19th-century Neo-Gothic mansion.

Left **La Barra, Punta del Este, Uruguay** Right **Plaza Independencia, Montevideo**

🔟 Best of the Rest

1 Barrio Histórico, Colonia
While one could cover historic Colonia in an afternoon, most visitors choose to linger long among its seven museums, perpetually blooming Plaza Mayor *(see p24)*, and wonderful sidewalk cafés. ✆ *Map B4*

2 Plaza Independencia, Montevideo
Tethering Montevideo to its long history, Plaza Independencia is overseen by Palacio Salvo, a mirror image of Palacio Barolo *(see p95)*. ✆ *Map B4*

3 Museo de ArteTigre, Tigre
This former casino, arguably the finest Beaux Arts structure in the country, today houses an excellent Argentinian art collection. ✆ *Map A4 • Paseo Victorica 972, Tigre • 4512-4528 • Open 9am–7pm Wed–Fri, noon–7pm Sat and Sun*

4 Casino Central, Mar del Plata
Constructed in the 1930s, the Casino Central might no longer evoke Monaco-on-the-Pampa, but it still is a notch above the typical beach-resort fare. ✆ *Map B6 • Bulevar Maritimo Peralta 2100 • 223-410-4450*

5 La Feria Mataderos
Dancers of all ages twirl to Argentina's other rhythm, *folclorica*, while onlookers quaff *chorizo* sandwiches at this Pampa-celebrating weekend fair *(see p97)*.

6 Centro Histórico, San Antonio de Areco
Impeccably preserved 19th-century Italianate municipal buildings, silversmiths, and *pulperías* testify to this once-crucial agricultural center's past fortunes. ✆ *Map A4*

7 La Barra, Punta del Este
At this point of land at La Barra, the most tranquil accommodations and most exclusive nightlife miraculously coexist. ✆ *Map C4*

8 Avenidas Bunge and del Mar, Pinamar
Pinamar's main thoroughfare, a tree-lined stretch of national-brand shopping, golf outfitters, and alfresco restaurants, terminates at the scenic shorefront of Avenida del Mar. ✆ *Map B5*

9 Presidential Residences, Isla Martín García
Ex-presidents who fell foul of the Argentinian government were imprisoned at the residences. Today they are remembered with commemorative plaques. ✆ *Map A4*

10 El Centinela, Tandil
The Mesozoic symbol of this mountain city is best appreciated from its neighboring hillside's peak, accessed by ski chairlift, where one can take in the view with a coffee and *alfajores (see p95)*. ✆ *Map A5*

El Drugstore, Colonia

Price Categories

For a three-course meal for one with half a bottle of wine (or equivalent meal), taxes, and extra charges.

$	under US$10
$$	US$11–15
$$$	US$16–25
$$$$	US$26–35
$$$$$	over US$35

🔟 Bars and Restaurants

El Drugstore, Colonia
A casual, exposed-kitchen gem covered with Warhol-inspired pop prints, El Drugstore serves tapas, cocktails, and *mate*. ✆ *Map B4 • Calle Vasconcellos 179 • 598-52-25241 • $$$*

El Mesón de la Plaza, Colonia
The most well-known restaurant in Colonia's Barrio Histórico, El Mesón has alfresco seating and an Uruguay-centric wine list to complement its grilled beef and lamb dishes. ✆ *Map B4 • Calle Vasconcellos 153 • 598-52-24807 • $$$*

Baar Fun Fun, Montevideo
A touchstone in tango lore, covered with clippings of illustrious musicians, Baar Fun Fun is also a great place for beer and a pizza. ✆ *Map Q5 • Calle Ciudadela 1229 • 598-291-58005 • $$$*

La Terraza, Tigre
Stop by for a filling menu of the usual meaty *parrilla* dishes. ✆ *Map B4 • Paseo Victorica 131 • 4731-2916 • $$$*

La Cuadrada, Mar del Plata
Find excellent teas, cakes, and home-made pastas at this fanciful eatery. ✆ *Map B6 • Avda. 9 de Julio 2737 • 0223-1557-05932 • $$$*

Vicente, Mataderos
The richer side of porteño cooking – roast chicken in spinach cream sauce and risotto with langoustines – competes with excellent *parrilla* fare at the convivial Vicente. ✆ *Map A4 • Avda. Escalada 2100 • 4635-4657 • $$$$*

Mi Vaca y Yo, Mataderos
The best place in Mataderos for *parrilla libre*, where waiters keep bringing little plates of requested cuts. The atmosphere can be hectic, but the meat is superb. ✆ *Map A4 • Calle Juan Felipe Aranguren 4201 • 4674-4878 • $$*

Lo de Charlie, Punta del Este
The intimate, pastel Lo de Charlie offers a warm, cozy sense of refinement. Excellent seafood dishes are prepared in the open kitchen, and the cheese ice cream is legendary. ✆ *Map C4 • Calle 9 & 12 • 598-424-44183 • $$$$$*

Tante, Pinamar
This bustling, handsome restaurant is popular for a group dinner or late-night drinks and fondue. German specialties feature alongside well-executed Argentinian classics like steaks and antipasti. ✆ *Map B5 • Calle de las Artes 35 • 02254-494949 • $$$$*

El Club, Tandil
The oil paintings and dark woods of a cigar lounge are mixed with checkerboard floors and small tables of a Parisian bistro, while the food and bar menus are suitably international. ✆ *Map A5 • Calle Pinto 636 • 02293-435878 • $$$$*

STREETSMART

General Information
102

Planning Your Trip
103

Getting to Buenos Aires
104

Getting Around
105

Things to Avoid
106

Budget Tips
107

Banking &
Communications
108

Security & Health
109

Shopping Tips
110

Accommodation &
Dining Tips
111

Places to Stay
112–117

BUENOS AIRES' TOP 10

Left **A tourist information center** Center **Disabled bathroom sign** Right **Local newspapers**

🔟 General Information

1 Tourist Information

There are tourist information desks at the city's international and domestic airports *(see p104)* and at locations throughout the city. Staff provide maps, general information, and accommodation advice. A complete list of information desks within the city can be found on the official tourist website www.bue.gov.ar.

2 Foreign Newspapers and Magazines

Foreign newspapers, *The Times* and *The New York Times*, as well as the magazines *Time* and *Newsweek* can be bought in Microcentro. Prices of these tend to be vastly inflated.

3 Local Newspapers and Magazines

The Buenos Aires Herald is an English-language daily, popular with expats and Anglo-Argentinians. It carries full event listings on Tuesday to Saturday. Of the Spanish-language dailies, *Clarín* and *La Nación* have listings sections on Fridays.

4 Free Publications and Listings

Published every two months, *The Argentina Independent* is a free English-language newspaper and is distributed in city bars, hotels, and hostels. *Wipe* is distributed all over the city and has full listings on music, club, bar, and restaurant scenes. *La Guia Divina* is distributed in San Telmo.

5 Websites

A good starting point is www.bue.gov.ar. Also try www.whatsupbuenos aires.com. For information on activities, shared housing, and jobs try www.yesba.org. For tango listings visit www.letstango.com.ar.

6 ASATEJ

The student travel agency, ASATEJ, has other uses besides flight reservations. It helps with language exchange requests and has details on housing. ◎ *Map Q5* • *3rd Floor, Office 320, Florida 835* • *4114-7528* • *Open 9am–7pm Mon–Fri* • *www.asatej.com*

7 Disabled Visitors

Only one subway line *(Línea H)* is equipped for wheelchair users *(Linea D is part-equipped)* and street ramps are in bad shape. Better hotels are equipped for disabled guests. City tours for wheelchair users are also available *(see p105)*.

8 Gay and Lesbian Travelers

Buenos Aires rivals Rio as South America's most prominent gay and lesbian destination. There is a gay pride festival in November, *Marcha del Orgullo Gay (see p43)* and numerous gay-oriented nightclubs and hangouts, although they tend to only get busy in the early hours *(see pp48–9)*. ◎ *Pride Travel: 2nd Floor, Office E, Paraguay 523* • *5218-6556* • *Open 10am–2pm, 3–6pm Mon–Fri* • *www.pride-travel.com*

9 Public Holidays

Public holidays are January 1 (New Year's Day); the second Mon and Tue in February (Carnaval); March 24 (National Day of Memory for Truth and Justice); March/April (dates vary: Holy Thursday; Good Friday); April 2 (Falklands/ Malvinas War Veterans Day); May 1 (Labor Day); May 25 (May Revolution Day); June 20 (Flag Day); July 9 (Independence Day); August 17 (San Martin Memorial Day); October 12 (Columbus Day); December 8 (Day of the Immaculate Conception); December 25 (Christmas).

10 Background Reads

For an overview of Argentina's history, pick up *The Argentina Reader* by Nouzeilles and Montaldo. Books on the Perón years include *Eva Perón* by Ortiz and *The Real Odessa* by Goñi. For lighter reading, the stunningly photographed *¡Tango!* by Collier and co-authors is a definitive guide. Miranda France's travelogue, *Bad Times in Buenos Aires*, is an account of an expat's life in the city in the 1990s.

 Preceding pages **Diners at Café Tortino**

Left **Tourists at the popular Reserva Ecológica Costanera Sur** Right **A currency exchange office**

🔟 Planning Your Trip

1 When to Go
The best time to visit Buenos Aires is during the southern hemisphere's spring or fall, when temperatures are a pleasant 64–73°F (18–23°C). In summer it can get hot and humid. In January and February, when temperatures reach 95°F (35°C), *porteños* leave the city en masse for Atlantic beach resorts.

2 What to Pack
In summer, pack light clothes, especially cotton and linen, since humidity reaches high levels. Also pack sunglasses, high-factor sunscreen, and a light raincoat. Heavy rain is common in January and February. In spring and fall, a light jacket and sweater will be needed, and in winter, a warm coat. Do pack some smart, stylish clothes too – *porteños* love to dress up when going out.

3 How Long to Stay
Allow at least a week for Buenos Aires. Seven days will give you enough time to explore the city's most important neighborhoods and sights, take in a tango show, and maybe squeeze in a day trip to Colonia in Uruguay too. Ten days to two weeks is ideal and will allow you to really get to know this amazing city – its stores, restaurants, parks, and other out-of-town attractions such as Tigre and San Antonio de Areco.

4 Passport and Visas
Citizens of the EU, the USA, and Canada do not require visas for Argentina. A 90-day entry permit is granted at immigration, which can be extended by a further 90 days on exiting the country or by paying a US$125 charge at the Dirección Nacional de Migraciones. US, Canadian, and Australian citizens must pay a reciprocity fee online before arrival. ◈ *Avda. Antártida Argentina 1355 Retiro • 4317-0200 • Open 8am–1:30pm Mon–Fri • www.migraciones.gov.ar*

5 Currency Information
The local currency is the Argentinian peso (AR$), divided into 100 centavos or cents. Bills are issued in 2-, 5-, 10-, 20-, 50-, and 100-peso denominations. Coins come in 1- and 2-peso and 5-, 10-, 25-, and 50-centavo denominations. The exchange rate hovers around AR$5 to US$1.

6 Health Preparations
No compulsory vaccinations are required for Buenos Aires and the city's tap water is safe to drink, though many visitors prefer bottled water. Visitors should take out their own medical insurance since Argentina does not have reciprocal health agreements with any other country.

7 Customs
Short-term visitors can bring the following items into Argentina without paying import duties: 11 lb (5 kg) of foodstuffs, 64 fl. oz. (2 l) of alcoholic drinks, 400 cigarettes, and 3.4 fl. oz. (100 ml) of perfume. Photographic equipment, medicine, and personal computers may also be imported duty-free.

8 Driver's Licenses
You can drive with a valid license issued from your own country, an international license is not necessary. Carry one other form of identification such as passport or national ID card whenever you drive.

9 Time Zone
Buenos Aires is 3 hours behind Greenwich Mean Time (GMT) during the summer and 4 hours behind GMT in the winter. It is 2 hours ahead of United States Eastern Standard time. Daylight Saving Time is not observed.

10 Electricity
Argentina uses a 220-volt, 50-cycle electrical system. Electrical sockets accept two- or three-pronged plugs. To use American appliances you will require a transformer and an adaptor, while British appliances need an adaptor only. Both can be bought at local hardware stores.

Southern hemisphere's seasons are: Spring: Sep–Nov; Summer: Dec–Feb; Fall: Mar–May; Winter: Jun–Aug

Left **A car rental sign in the city** Right **Planes at the airport**

⓾ Getting to Buenos Aires

1 By Air
Aerolíneas Argentinas flies directly to Buenos Aires from Europe and North America. Several European carriers also fly directly to Buenos Aires, including Air France (from Paris), Alitalia (from Milan and Rome), Iberia (from Barcelona and Madrid), and Lufthansa (from Frankfurt). British Airways flies direct from London. From the USA, American and United have non-stop services.

2 Aeropuerto Ministro Pistarini
Buenos Aires' international airport is Aeropuerto Ministro Pistarini, commonly called Ezeiza after the district in which it is located. Nearly all international flights arrive at terminal A or B. Ezeiza is located 1 hour from downtown Buenos Aires. ◉ *For recorded flight information on international and domestic flights: 5480-6111; www.aa2000.com.ar*

3 By Shuttle or Bus from Ezeiza
With sales desks in Terminals A and B, Manuel Tienda León runs a 24-hour shuttle service between Ezeiza and the city center. Mini-buses are modern and air-conditioned and depart from Ezeiza every half hour for the company's downtown office. From there, a connecting service takes visitors to hotels. One public bus, line 86, runs between Ezeiza and the city center. ◉ *Avda. E. Madero 1299; 0810 888-5366; www.tiendaleon.com.ar*

4 By Taxi or *Remis* from Ezeiza
Unauthorized taxi and *remis* (mini-cab) drivers swarm the terminal exits at Ezeiza and are best avoided. Instead, order a taxi from one of the approved firms operating from within the airport or phone to arrange your own taxi.

5 Aeroparque Jorge Newbery
The city's domestic airport is Aeroparque Jorge Newbery and is located in the city's Palermo district 10 minutes from downtown. It handles almost all domestic flights, plus flights to and from Uruguay and Brazil.

6 By Shuttle or Bus
From Aeroparque Manuel Tienda León runs a shuttle service between the domestic airport and the city center, departing every half-hour. Several public bus lines also connect Aeroparque with the city center.

7 By Taxi or *Remise* from Aeroparque
Taxis line up at the exit to the arrivals area. You can also hire a taxi or *remise* from one of the approved firms operating from within the airport, or call one of your own. ◉ *Radio Taxis: Mi Taxi 4931-1200 • Remises: Blue 4777-8888*

8 By Long-Distance Bus
Buses arriving in Buenos Aires from interior provinces or from neighboring countries stop at the city's central bus terminal, the Estación Terminal de Omnibus, commonly called Retiro. There are connections from Retiro to local bus services. ◉ *Avda. Ramos Mejía 1680; 4310-0707*

9 By Boat
Frequent ferries from Montevideo and Colonia in Uruguay, and one ferry from Punta del Este arrive several times daily at the Dársena Norte (Northern Dock) boat terminal in the Puerto Madero district. ◉ *Avda. Antártida Argentina 821; Ticket sales: 4316-6500*

10 Car Rental
Avis and Hertz have their offices in the airports. Prices vary, but a rough guide is US$150 per day for a medium-sized car, depending on required mileage. To rent a car, you must be over 21 and have a driver's license, a credit card, and a passport. ◉ *Avis: 0810 9991-2847; www.avis.com.ar • Hertz: 4816 8001; www.hertz.com*

The city's subway system runs from 5am to 11pm Mon–Sat and 8am to 10pm Sun.

Left **A bus on the city streets** Center **A cyclist at Parque 3 de Febrero** Right **A subway sign**

🔟 Getting Around

1 Bus
Buenos Aires is well-serviced by bus routes, even if the buses (called *colectivos* in Spanish) do nothing for the city's noise and pollution levels. For bus stops and routes, buy a copy of *Guía T* from a kiosk or, better still, ask a local. The standard fare for journeys of any length is AR$2, payable in coins into the ticket machine behind the driver's seat.

2 Subway
The Buenos Aires subway system is a safe, reliable, and good way of getting around central districts. There are six lines: A, B, C, D, E, and H. Line A is the oldest (and still uses wooden trains) and Line D, which links Microcentro with Palermo, is busiest. The standard fare per journey is AR$2.50. Tickets covering up to 10 journeys can be bought at stations.

3 Tram
Inaugurated in 2007, the Tranvía del Este serves the Puerto Madero district, running parallel to Avenida Alicia Moreau de Justo between Avenidas Córdoba and Independencia.

4 Train
Trains heading north from Buenos Aires, including those stopping at Tigre, depart from Retiro, train station located adjacent to the Retiro bus terminal. Trains departing for destinations south of the capital, such as Tandil, Pinamar, and Mar del Plata, depart from Constitución station. Of these two lines, the northern line is safer and more modern.

5 Taxi and *Remis*
Taxis are ubiquitous in Buenos Aires. Standard taxis and radio taxis are both recognizable by their yellow-and-black coloring. Radio taxis, recognizable by "radio taxi" written on their doors, are safer and can be both flagged at street level or ordered by phone. *Remises* (private taxi companies with unmarked cars) can be hired by phone or from street offices.

6 Driving
Driving in the city is a nightmare. Traffic is heavy, local driving habits are risky, and parking is scarce. Add a maze of one-way systems and driving becomes even more challenging. If you do drive, remember that cars crossing from the right have right of way, and the speed limit is 25 mph (40km/h) rising to 37 mph (60km/h) on main avenues.

7 Bicycling
On the road, potholes and drivers' general lack of respect for two-wheelers make cycling dangerous. Enjoy safe cycling in Parque 3 de Febrero *(see p61)*, and in the Puerto Madero and Recoleta districts, or on the many cycle lanes. Rent bikes at park entrances.

8 On Foot
The best way to explore Buenos Aires is on foot. Distances between neighborhoods are short and easy to navigate. Microcentro is best avoided on weekdays.

9 Transport for Disabled Travelers
For disabled travelers, QRV – Transportes Especiales runs tailor-made city tours in modern wheelchair-equipped vehicles. ✆ *QRV– Transportes Especiales: 4306-6635*

10 Guided Tours
Eternautas runs historical tours and Opción Sur specializes in audio-visual tours. Tangol offers soccer game visits and helicopter tours. Bike Tours runs bicycling excursions. Free guided tours are available *(see p107)* and Buenos Tours specializes in private walking tours with native English-speaking guides. ✆ *Eternautas: 5031-9916; www.eternautas.com • Opción Sur: 4777-9029; www.opcionsur.com.ar • Tangol: 4312-7276; www.tangol.com • Bike Tours: 4311-5199; www.biketours.com.ar •Buenos Tours: 3221-1048;www.buenostours.com*

Left **Heavy traffic on Avenida Corrientes** Right **Crowds in San Telmo**

🔟 Things to Avoid

1 Tourist Traps
Avoid the costly leather goods stores on Calle Florida and the herd 'em in herd 'em out "tango for export" shows aimed at visitors. Give a wide berth to the over-priced Irish theme pubs in Microcentro since they are neither authentic Irish nor Argentinian. Think twice before spending money on second-rate steak at expensive and characterless restaurants in Puerto Madero.

2 Crime Hotspots
Buenos Aires is generally a very safe city but be careful in certain areas. These include the southern districts of La Boca and Constitución. In San Telmo watch out for pickpockets and "mustard" scams – a local trick in which mustard or other liquids are squirted over your shirt on a busy street. A "passerby" brings it to your attention and helps you wipe it off, just as a third person uses the distraction to nab your wallet.

3 Rush Hour
Traffic in Buenos Aires is heavy, with rush hour lasting nearly all day. Roads are worse on weekdays before 10am and between 5pm and 8pm, especially on Friday evenings, when middle-class *porteños* leave the city en masse for weekend houses in Buenos Aires' province.

4 Taking a Taxi Without Change
If you offer high deno-mination notes, the driver will spend 15 minutes driving around looking for change, while adding to your fare. It's a good idea to check beforehand if the driver is carrying change, or in the case of radio taxis, inform the operator. Radio taxis charge a call-up fee of AR$5.

5 Unscrupulous Taxi Drivers
Never get into a taxi that does not display an official registration certificate on the back of the driver's or front passenger's seat. Avoid flagging down taxis in the Puerto Madero district, where rogue taxis circulate.

6 Dog Poop
Dog poop here features as a major issue in mayoral elections, alongside unemployment and crime. It is especially bad in residential districts such as San Telmo and Palermo Viejo, where it is strongly advised that you keep your eyes fixed to the ground and watch where you are walking.

7 Parque 3 de Febrero at Night
Beautiful by day, Parque 3 de Febrero turns dark at night – literally and metaphorically. This is when the city's transvestite prostitutes and their pimps take over. While some visitors will wish to avoid it, others may want to take the sight in.

8 Unauthorized Money Changers
Called *arbolitos* or "little trees," these have lined Calle Florida since Argentina's 2001 eco-nomic crisis. They are likely to rip you off on the exchange rate or give you fake peso notes.

9 Taking Offense
Porteños pay little heed to political correctness. Young and old swear with gay abandon. Despite a ban on smoking in public places, smokers are everywhere. And it is a relentlessly macho society in which women travelers can be subjected to passing comments. However, it is all invariably harmless, and best taken with a large pinch of salt.

10 January
Not the best month to visit Buenos Aires. This is when tempera-tures reach 104°F (40°C) and humidity soars. The city's cultural activities and nightlife also take a dip since most *porteños* leave the city for vacations, heading to Argentina's Atlantic coast resorts. On the flip side, hotel prices at this time are cheap.

Left **Teatro San Martín** Center **Antigua Tasca de Cuchilleros sign** Right **Centro Cultural Recoleta**

🔟 Budget Tips

Cheap Eats
Decent cheap eats can be had at *tenedor libres* (all you can eat), where a buffet meal for one costs US$5. Most are concentrated in Microcentro; look out for a *tenedor libre* sign in the window. For nutritious bites, every *porteño* neighborhood has its own *bodegón*, a family-oriented steakhouse which serves large and inexpensive steak dishes.

Cheap Nights Out
Most bars offer happy hour drinks between 6 and 10pm. Switch to cheaper local beer after that, the most popular of which is Quilmes. Fernet, a spirit usually mixed with coke, is equally inexpensive and popular.

Free Parks and Gardens
Buenos Aires has free parks and gardens that are perfect for walking, sunbathing, and playing sports. Among the most popular ones are the Reserva Ecológica Costanera Sur, an ecological preserve to the east of Puerto Madero; Palermo's Jardín Botánico Carlos Thays (Botanical Garden); and Parque 3 de Febrero.

Free Museums and Galleries
Many museums and galleries offer free entry throughout the week, including the Museo de Bellas Artes *(see pp16–17)* and the Museo de la Casa Rosada *(see p8)*. Some allow free entry once a week. Discounts are available for students with valid ID and people over 65.

Free Cultural Events
"Gallery Nights," held from March to November on the last Friday of the month, between 7 and 11pm, sees over 60 art galleries offering entry for free. The annual Noche de los Museos in October sees more than 100 museums offering free entry. In the summer months, look out for free classical music concerts held on weekends in Palermo's Parque Rosedal, as well as Carnaval celebrations in February. ◎ *Gallery Nights: www.gallery-nights.com.ar • Noche de los Museos: www.lanochedelosmuseos. com.ar*

Free Tours
The city government runs free guided visits to historically important neighborhoods and buildings, and themed tours on personalities such as Evita and Borges. Check the official tourist website *(see p102)*, which also has downloadable city-audio tours in English and Spanish. For more free guided tours, contact Cicerones, a non-government organization that works with over 70 bilingual guides. Simply fill out the online form. ◎ *www.cicerones.org.ar*

Cheap Stays
Hostels are your best bet for cheap stays. Many have double and twin rooms available at modest rates. You will also benefit from the use of the kitchen, fridge, laundry, and lounge areas *(see p117)*.

Launderettes
Launderettes are very cheap and ubiquitous, found everywhere along side streets off main avenues. A same-day service for a large bag of clothing typically costs around US$5 to wash and tumble-dry. Ask at your hotel reception for the nearest launderette.

Cheap Movies and Theater
Movie theater tickets are half-price from Monday to Wednesday and for mid-day and afternoon screenings throughout the week. State-run stage theaters offer discounted entry once a week.

Picnics
Buying lunch every day can be expensive. Instead, store bread, fruit, cheese, and cold meats in the fridge at your place of accommodation and pack lunch for the day. You can safely drink tap water.

Left **Banco Francés** Center **ATM** Right **Locutorio and Internet Café**

🔟 Banking & Communications

Banks
Banks generally open 10am–3pm on weekdays, though some may open an hour earlier or close an hour later. Currency exchange counters within banks tend to offer better exchange and commission rates than an exchange bureau, although rates vary from bank to bank. All banks are equipped with ATM machines; just look for the "Link" sign that shows they accept foreign bank cards.

ATMs
ATMs provide the easiest way to access money, although there is a $300 limit per transaction and the bank in Argentina will charge a withdrawal fee. Nearly all of them accept Visa, MasterCard, and American Express cards and operate 24 hours. Surcharges depend on your bank.

Credit Cards
The most widely accepted credit and debit cards in Buenos Aires are Visa and MasterCard and to a lesser extent, American Express and Diner's Club. ◈ *In case of stolen credit cards call: American Express 0810-555-2639 • MasterCard 0800-555-0507 • Visa 4379-3333 • Diners Club (Citi) 0810-444-2484*

Changing Money
There are numerous currency exchange bureaux *(casas de cambio)* in Microcentro, on Florida, Sarmiento, and San Martín streets in particular. They are open 9am–3pm daily. Commission rates at banks tend to be lower.

Traveler's Checks
Traveler's checks can always be changed at banks or a currency exchange bureau, but at high rates of commission, often as much as 3 percent. The American Express office however, cashes its own traveler's checks free of charge. Note that businesses other than a currency exchange bureau rarely accept traveler's checks under any circumstance. ◈ *American Express: Arenales 707; 0810-444-2437*

Bank Transfers
Sending money from overseas can be done via Western Union. Visit their website for charges, maximum payments, and a list of local affiliates. ◈ *www.westernunion.com*

Mail
Branches of the Correo Argentino postal service are open 9am–6pm on weekdays and they send airmail by general delivery as well as registered post *(correo certificado)*. *Poste Restante* mail should be sent to the city's central post office and addressed as follows: Recipient's name, Lista de Correos: Correo Central, Sarmiento 189, (1003) Capital Federal, Argentina. Telephone call centers undertake airmailing too, but by general delivery only. ◈ *Correo Argentino: www.correoargentino.com.ar*

Telephone and Fax
Call centers *(locutorios)* are ubiquitous in Buenos Aires, and telecom giants Telefónica and Telecom are the two largest operators. Most centers are open 10am–11pm daily and all offer international call and fax services.

Cell Phones
Most foreign cell phones work in Argentina with a tri-band or quad-band, but making calls can be expensive, and receiving calls and text difficult. You can use your own phone and buy a local SIM card, which can be bought at kiosks for around US$2.50. Renting a cell phone is a good alternative. ◈ *Mobile Phone Rental: San Martín 948, 3rd floor; 4311-2933; www.phonerental.com.ar*

Internet Access
Call centers and Internet cafés provide Internet access and both are found at almost every turn in Buenos Aires. Service is via speedy broadband connection and is usually very cheap. Most modern bars, cafés, and restaurants have wireless connections.

When calling Buenos Aires from overseas, dial +5411 before the local 8-digit number. When calling from Argentina, first dial 011.

Left **Dental care** Center **Policeman** Right **Farmacia de La Estrella**

🔟 Security & Health

1 Emergency Numbers

In case of emergency the following numbers can be dialed free of charge 24 hours a day. ✪ *Policía* (police) 911 • *Bomberos* (fire service) 100 • *Emergencia médica* (ambulance service) 107 • *Defensa Civil* (for gas leaks, power cuts, flooding) 103

2 Police

Should you be unfortunate enough to be a victim of crime, report the incident at the *Comisaría del Turista*, located downtown. Specifically for tourists, it is staffed with English-speaking police 24 hours a day. Otherwise go directly to the nearest police station or *comisaría*. ✪ *Comisaría del Turista: Avda. Corrientes 436; 0800-999-5000; open 24hrs; turista@ policiafederal.gov.ar*

3 Theft Prevention

Buenos Aires is extremely safe when compared to other Latin American cities and most big cities anywhere in the world. Most crimes can be avoided by taking a few simple precautions. Never leave bags unattended or on the back of chairs in bars and restaurants, do not flash money or mobile phones around, do not show off expensive photographic or video equipment, and avoid crime hotspots *(see p106).*

4 Taking Taxis

The safest way is to phone a radio taxi or *remise (see p105).* If you do flag a taxi at street level, look for a radio taxi ("radio taxi" is written on the car doors) rather than a standard taxi, as it is safer. This is especially advisable in Puerto Madero where rogue taxis are known to circulate. Also, never take a taxi from directly outside an ATM; walk a couple of blocks first.

5 Hospitals and Medical Clinics

Medical treatment is best sought at one of the city's private hospitals, where the cost of treatment is low compared to the USA and Europe, and the level of service high. Hospital Británico has a main hospital in the south of the city for 24-hour emergencies and neighborhood clinics for medical consultations. ✪ *Map D5; Hospital Británico: Perdriel 74; 4309-6400; www. hospitalbritanico.org.ar*

6 Dental Treatment

Dental treatment in Buenos Aires is good and inexpensive and most private hospitals have dental clinics. For emergencies, the Servicio de Urgencias, at the state university's dental faculty, is open 24 hours a day. ✪ *Servicio de Urgencias; Marcelo T de Alvear 2146; 4964-1259*

7 Pharmacies

Argentina's biggest pharmacy chain is Farmacity, which has branches throughout the city. All neighborhoods have access to 24-hour pharmacies. Head to the nearest one; if it is not open, the address of the nearest *farmacia de turno* will be posted on its door. It is usually just a couple of blocks away.

8 Drinking Water

Argentina's tap water is safe to drink. Many visitors, however, prefer to drink bottled water.

9 Women Travelers

Most women travelers will find Buenos Aires a relaxed and casual city. Argentinian men can sometimes be over amorous, but this is easily deflected with a firm *estoy casada* ("I'm married"). Women travelers should, however, take care when taking taxis alone and should always phone a radio taxi.

10 Consulates

Most major countries have consulates in the city. In an emergency, especially if you have any dealings with the police, insist on contacting your consulate. ✪ *Consulates:* • Australia 4779-3550 • Canada 4808-1000 • Ireland 5787-0801 • New Zealand 4328-0747 • UK 4808-2200 • USA 5777-4533

Left **An item at an antique shop** Center **Leather items on display** Right **Bookstore**

TOP10 Shopping Tips

1 Opening Hours
Shopping malls are usually open 10am–10pm though there may be an hour's variation. Food courts and movie theaters within malls stay open longer. Other stores open 9am–8pm Monday to Friday, though weekend hours vary. Some close at 1pm on Saturday or all day Sunday.

2 Taxes and Refunds
Argentina's sales tax of 21 percent is included in the advertised price for goods. Visitors can claim back the tax on any purchases with a Global Refund logo when buying Argentinian-manufactured products above AR$70 (US$15). Ask for a receipt and Global Refund check when making a purchase. On leaving Argentina these are stamped at Customs, which sends you to an airport *puesto de pago* (payment counters) for a refund.

3 Payment
Cash, preferably the Argentinian peso, is accepted in most stores though many places also accept US dollars. Credit cards are usually accepted, except in small stores. Preferred cards are Visa and MasterCard, American Express, and Diner's Club *(see p108)*.

4 Shopping Zones
It is crowded and traffic-choked, but Microcentro should still be the starting point for shoppers, especially the pedestrian Calle Florida. There is a bit of everything here, from malls and department stores to artisans' shops. Recoleta has high-end boutiques with local and international labels. Trendy Palermo Viejo has many boho-chic clothes stores.

5 Leather Goods
Argentinian leather is of excellent quality and favorably priced compared to Europe and the USA. Stores sell leather goods, though those on Calle Florida can be overpriced. The leather shops at the intersection of Murillo and Scalabrini Ortíz in Palermo offer the best deals.

6 Souvenirs
For gaucho ware, traditional *maté* paraphernalia, and indigenous woolens, try stores such as El Boyero, Kelly's, and Mission *(see p38)*. You can buy inexpensive handicrafts at the weekend artisans' fair at Plaza Francia in Recoleta *(see p36)*. For tango memorabilia, head to the stores on Avenida Corrientes.

7 Antiques
San Telmo is famous for its antique stores and fair, held each Sunday at Plaza Dorrego *(see p18)*. Mercado de las Pulgas in Palermo Viejo is a good flea market. ⊕ *Mercado de las Pulgas: Avda. Dorrego y Álvarez Thomas*

8 Argentinian Wine
Found in shopping zones and malls, *Vinotecas* (or wine boutiques) stock wines from Argentina's wine growing regions, including Mendoza. Ligier and Terroir offer packaging and delivery services. ⊕ *Ligier: Map Q5; Avda. Sante Fe 800; 5353-8060; www.ligier.com.ar • Terroir: Map L1; Buschiazzo 3040; 4778-3443; www.terroir. com.ar*

9 Music
Local mega-chain Musimundo has many branches in the city. Its collection includes Argentinian rock and folk music. Zival's *(see p27)* offers tango, jazz, and classical. Disquería Bird and Abraxas feature vinyl. ⊕ *Musimundo: Avda. Santa Fe 1844; www. musimundo.com; Disquería Bird: Talcahuano 385; 4382-2539; Abraxas: Galería 5ta Avda.; Avda. Santa Fe 1270*

10 Books
The glorious Ateneo Grand Splendid, the largest bookstore in South America, stocks English-language books. Otherwise, try Gandhi Galerna *(see p69)*. Find second-hand English-language books at Walrus Books. ⊕ *Ateneo Grand Splendid: Avda. Santa Fe 1860; 4811-6104; www. elateneo.com; Walrus Books: Estados Unidos 617, 4300-7135; www.walrus-books.com.ar*

For Buenos Aires' best shopping malls **See p39.**

Left **Boutique Home Hotel in Palermo** Right **Cabaña Las Lilas restaurant**

🔟 Accommodation & Dining Tips

1 Choosing Hotel Locations

Microcentro offers proximity to the main shopping district, but can be crowded by day and seedy at night. Upscale districts Recoleta and Puerto Madero, close to the city center, are quieter, and more pleasant alternatives. Both have several luxury hotels, and Recoleta also has excellent mid-range options. Both San Telmo and Palermo Viejo have good boutique hotel, B&B, and hostel options. For history, try San Telmo, and for proximity to shopping and dining, Palermo Viejo.

2 Seasonal Demand

The high season is July–August with several national holidays and winter school vacations. Easy availability of rooms and cheap rates are possible January–February, when *porteños* escape to coastal resorts and business travel slows to a near halt.

3 Rack Rates

The rack rates provided in this book are for the high season and aim at providing a guide price. However, it is possible to get a better deal as rates vary according to season, time of week, length of stay, and how you make your reservation. Sales tax, at a whopping 21 percent in Argentina, should be included in a hotel's quoted rate, but double-check when booking. Hotel rates quoted in this guide include tax.

4 Longer-Stay Options

Several agencies specialize in short- and long-term rentals of furnished apartments. Buenos Aires Travel Rent and Buenos Aires Stay each have over 100 apartments to rent. ✆ *Buenos Aires Travel Rent: 4371-2424; www.buenosaires travelrent.com • Buenos Aires Stay: 5365-0238; www.buenosairesstay.com*

5 Traveling with Kids

Most hotels allow children under 12 to stay with their parents free of charge by adding a bed to a double room or arranging a triple room with double and single beds.

6 Restaurant Reservations

Book ahead when dining out in Buenos Aires, especially on weekends. Give one or two days' notice, rising to three or four for the exclusive restaurants. If asked for a number when making a reservation, your hotel number should suffice.

7 Meal Times

Porteños stop for lunch around 1pm, dip into a café for coffee and pastries around 5pm, and then have a late evening meal at around 9–10pm, and as late as 11pm on weekends. Accordingly, restaurants open noon–4pm and 8pm–1am. Kitchens stop taking orders an hour prior to closing time.

8 The Menu and Ordering

Increasingly, menus are written in both Spanish and English. If you don't understand an item, just ask a waiter. Many restaurants have "executive menus" aimed at the lunchtime crowd and featuring a three-course meal and a drink at a fixed price. In steakhouses, ask for your steak to come *jugoso* (rare), *a punto* (medium-rare), or *bien cocido* (well -done). For wines, ask for either *vino tinto* (red) or *vino blanco* (white).

9 Dress Codes

Though most restaurants do not enforce dress codes, many diners choose to dress well for a night at upscale restaurants. Some nightclubs will not permit entrance if you wear sneakers.

10 Tipping

Tipping in the city is in proportion with most other cities. Hotel porters are given a *propina* (tip) of around US$2–3. For the waiting staff in hotel restaurants tip 10–15 percent of the bill. On checking out, leave a tip for the maids.

➜ *For more on the best restaurants in Buenos Aires* **See pp56–7.**

Left **Four Seasons Hotel** Center **725 Continental Hotel** Right **Restaurant at Faena Hotel**

🔟 Luxury Hotels

1 Alvear Palace Hotel

The Alvear is the city's most luxurious hotel. Its suites boast antique art, Egyptian linen, and butler service. Luxuriate in the marbled wellness spa, and enjoy the lavish restaurants. ⍟ Map P4 • Avda. Alvear 1891, Recoleta • 4808-2100 • www.alvearpalace.com • $$$$$

2 Four Seasons Hotel

Stay in a standard room in the elegant main tower, with king-sized beds and marble furnishings, or at the six-suited mansion. Another feature is a classical garden with a Roman pool. ⍟ Map P4 • Posadas 1086/88, Recoleta • 4321-1200 • www.fourseasons. com • $$$$$

3 Park Hyatt Buenos Aires

The contemporary suites of this restored 1930s palace contrast with the classic splendor of its public spaces. Luxurious amenities here include a wellness center, private garden, underground art gallery, and indoor pool. ⍟ Map P4 • Avda. Alvear 1661, Recoleta • 5171-1234 • www.buenosaires.park. hyatt.com • $$$$$

4 Caesar Park

This glossy, modern tower's suites are spacious, thickly carpeted, and embellished by marble and hardwood furnishings. It also has a business center, a spa and pool, restaurant, and a Japanese garden. ⍟ Map P4 • Posadas 1232, Recoleta • 4819-1100 • www.caesar-park.com • $$$$$

5 Faena Hotel and Universe

The Faena offers rock-star luxury for the ultra-hip and loaded. Its interior is a lavish blend of romance and razor-sharp modernity. Guests also get an "Experience Manager." There is a pool, gym, spa, cabaret theater, and a wine cellar. ⍟ Map G2 • Martha Salotti 445, Dique 2, Puerto Madero Este • 4010-9000 • www.faenahoteland universe.com • $$$$$

6 Hotel Madero

Hotel Madero features a rooftop pool with a retractable roof and panoramic river-city vistas. Rooms are stylish and every amenity imaginable is provided. ⍟ Map G3 • Rosario Vera Peñaloza 360, Dique 2, Puerto Madero Este • 5776-7777 • www.hotel madero.com • $$$$$

7 Sofitel Buenos Aires

A hotel to fall in love with, the Sofitel is a 1929 Art Deco building. Its lobby, with checkerboard floor, huge Art Deco chandelier, and a vast skylight, dazzles.

Botticino bathrooms, an aromatic spa, and a Roman pool round off the seduction. ⍟ Map Q4 • Arroyo 841, Retiro • 4131-0000 • www.sofitelbuenos aires.com.ar • $$$$$

8 Marriott Plaza Hotel

A beautiful Belle Époque building with elegant suites and roof-top spa. The Plaza Bar here is a great place for a tranquil pre-dinner cocktail. ⍟ Map Q5 • Florida 1005, Retiro • 4318-3000 • www.marriottplaza. com.ar • $$$$$

9 Axel Hotel

Latin America's first five-star gay hotel, "hetero-friendly" Axel is a hip crash pad. Facilities include a rooftop pool, garden, gym, solarium, health and cocktail bars, and a stylish restaurant. Friday-night DJ parties welcome non-guests. ⍟ Map F2 • Venezuela 649, San Telmo • 4136-9393 • www.axelhotels.com • $$$

10 725 Continental Hotel

Behind the classical French façade lies a modern interior with innovative design. State-of-the-art facilities include a rooftop pool, spa, and business and fitness centers. ⍟ Map Q6 • Avda. Roque Sáenz Peña 725, Microcentro • 4131-8000 • www.725 continental.com • $$$

Almost all hotels accept credit cards, have en suite bathrooms, and air conditioning.

562 Nogaró

🔟 High-End & Business Hotels

1 Hilton Buenos Aires

The super-slick Hilton's standard rooms feature ergonomic chairs and Puerto Madero or River Plate vistas. Amenities include a fitness center, outdoor pool, wine bar, international restaurant, and business facilities. ✪ Map G1 • Macacha Guemes 351, Dique 3, Puerto Madero Este • 4891-0000 • www.hilton.com • $$$$$

2 Sheraton Buenos Aires Hotel and Convention Center

This centrally located hotel's standard doubles are spacious and sound-proofed and have river or city views. It has superb business facilities, an international restaurant, a shopping arcade with beauty salon and art gallery, indoor and outdoor pool, tennis courts, a gym, and spa. ✪ Map Q4 • San Martín 1225/1275, Retiro • 4318-9000 • www.sheraton-ba.com • $$$$

3 Claridge Hotel

Rooms at the English Claridge have hardwood workstations and antique mirrors and picture frames. Enjoy too its Tudor-styled restaurant, outdoor heated pool, gym, sauna, and spa. The business center provides bilingual secretaries. ✪ Map Q5 • Tucumán 535, Microcentro • 4314-8022 • www.claridge.com.ar • $$$

4 Pestana Buenos Aires

Four blocks from the Obelisco, facilities include a large indoor pool, gym, and spa. Rooms are generously sized and soundproofed. Close to the financial district. ✪ Map Q5 • Carlos Pellegrini 877, Retiro • 5239-1000 • www.pestana.com • $$$

5 NH City and Tower

A restored 1930s Art Deco building, NH City and Tower is one block away from Plaza de Mayo. Amenities include business center, gym, and sauna. The 12th-floor roof-terrace pool has river-skyscraper views. ✪ Map F2 • Bolívar 160, Monserrat • 4121-6464 • www.nh-hoteles.com • $$$

6 Hotel Emperador

This hotel blends classic design with state-of-the-art technology. Rooms are king-sized and have panoramic river vista or intimate views of a private garden. Facilities include a spa, fitness center, indoor pool, and gourmet restaurant. ✪ Map Q4 • Avda. del Libertador 420, Retiro • 4131-4000 • www.hotelemperador.com.ar • $$$

7 Dazzler Tower

The superbly located Dazzler has 11 floors of understated, stylishly furnished, soundproofed rooms: ask for one on floors 9–11 for sunrise views of the River Plate. Facilities include a spa, pool, and gym. Suites include a Jacuzzi. ✪ Map Q5 • San Martín 920, Retiro • 5217-5793 • www.dazzlertower.com • $$$$$

8 Intercontinental Buenos Aires

This hotel has a state-of-the-art fitness center, solarium, indoor heated pool, spa, and spacious, modern elegant rooms. Plus a business center, executive lounges, and an international restaurant. ✪ Map E2 • Moreno 809, Monserrat • 4340-7100 • www.buenos-aires.intercontinental.com • $$$$$

9 Design Suites

The Zen tranquility of the lobby sets the tone at this sleek design hotel with minimalist decor. Suites include music systems, hydromassage baths, DVD players, and balconies according to category. ✪ Map N5 • Marcelo T. de Alvear 1683, Barrio Norte • 4814-8700 • www.designsuites.com • $$

🔟 562 Nogaró Buenos Aires

At the cheaper end of its price category, services here include business and fitness centers. A standard room has a parquet floor, a queen-sized bed, a work station, and Wi-Fi broadband. ✪ Map F2 • Avda. Julio A. Roca 562, Monserrat • 4331-0091 • www.562nogarohotel.com • $$$

Room rates may vary with season, availability, specials, and promotions. All prices listed are high-season rack rates.

113

Left **Home Hotel** Center **Krista Hotel Boutique** Right **Mansión Dandi Royal**

TOP 10 Boutique Hotels

1 Esplendor de Buenos Aires

A stunning Belle Époque building, the Esplendor's stylish bar-restaurant and spacious rooms are contemporary. But its best feature is the huge pop-icon mosaics that line the corridors, including one of Che Guevara. Map Q5 • San Martín 780, Microcentro • 5173-3601 • www.esplendorbuenos aires.com • $$$$$

2 Meliá Recoleta Plaza

The Meliá offers five-star luxury in a boutique package. Suites are lavishly decorated in the Louis XV style. Amenities include business/fitness centers, spa with exterior Jacuzzi, and a sumptuous restaurant with terrace. Map P4 • Posadas 1557, Recoleta • 5353-4000 • www.solmelia.com• $$$$

3 Art Hotel

This 100-year-old town house combines boutique style with accessible rates. There are 36 classically decorated rooms, a cozy living area, well-stocked library, business lounge, patio and sun-drenched roof garden, and art gallery. Map N4 • Azcuenaga 1268 • 4821-4744 • www. arthotel.com.ar • $$$

4 La Cayetana Historic House

Set in a restored 1820s home, La Cayetana's 11 spacious rooms boast lovely design touches. Living and dining areas open onto two Italianate courtyards and a garden. Map E2 • México 1330, Monserrat • 4383-2230 • www.lacayetanahotel. com.ar • $$

5 Moreno 376

In this 1929 Art Deco building, all suites blend contemporary cool with Art Deco detail. The modern Latin-American restaurant, bijou jazz/tango theater, gym and roof-terrace with Jacuzzi and cupola-and-turret vistas, complete the package. Map F2 • Moreno 376, Monserrat • 6091-2000 • www.morenobueno saires.com • $$$$

6 Mansión Dandi Royal

Tango-themed Dandi Royal is a century-old mansion house with beautifully restored Art Nouveau interior. Tango murals and objet d'art decorate the 30 rooms. Amenities include a gym, a rooftop pool, solariums, and a mini-spa. Three tango salons host shows and classes. Map E3 • Piedras 922/936, San Telmo • 4307-7623 • www.man siondandiroyal.com • $$

7 Home Hotel Buenos Aires

Home mixes luxury with informality. A minimalist interior is infused with funky flourishes. Suites are sublimely appointed with custom-made bath amenities. Unwind in the spa, garden, or pool. Map J2 • Honduras 5860, Palermo Viejo • 4778-1008 • www.homebuenos aires.com • $$$$

8 Krista Hotel Boutique

This romantic hideaway is a restored 1920s home with an elaborate lounge and spacious suites. There are three patios and a massage-therapy salon. Ideal for the visiting couple. Map J3 • Bonpland 1665, Palermo Viejo • 4771-4697 • www. kristahotel.com.ar • $$$$

9 Fierro

This high-end option has spacious suites, complete with pillow and wine menus. The rooftop plunge pool is perfect to cool off in. Gourmands will enjoy a visit to the hotel's HG Restaurant (see p93). Great breakfasts, too. Map J2 • Soler 5862 • 3220-6800 • www.fierrohotel. com • $$$

10 Casa Las Cañitas

This chic hotel sits on a quiet street in Las Cañitas. The interior is bright, contemporary, and subtly stylish, and features nine rooms, plus a lounge area and resto-bar. Communal space includes a roof terrace and Zen garden with a sun deck. Map K1 • Huergo 283, Las Cañitas • 4771-3878 • www.casalas canitas.com • $$$

Carsson Hotel

Price Categories

For a standard,	**$** under US$50
double room per	**$$** US$50–110
night (with breakfast	**$$$** US$110–170
if included), taxes,	**$$$$** US$170–240
and extra charges.	**$$$$$** over US$240

🔟 Mid-Range Hotels

1 Hotel Colón
In this hotel, doubles are modern, sound-proofed, and painted in relaxing neutral tones. There is a pool, gym, and international restaurant. Ask for a room with a view of Avenida 9 de Julio. 🕙 Map P6 • Carlos Pellegrini 507, Microcentro • 4320-3500 • www.hotel colon.com.ar • $$$

2 Ulises Recoleta Suites
Each suite in this intimate hotel has a kitchenette and can be shared by up to three people. It's an affordable option in the city's most upmarket neighborhood. 🕙 Map P4 • Ayacucho 2016, Recoleta • 4804-4571 • www.ulisesrecoleta.com. ar • $$$

3 Rendez-Vous
This delightful boutique hotel dates from 1904 and has eleven individually furnished rooms. It is in a great location in the center of Palermo Hollywood. 🕙 Map J3 • Bonpland 1484, Palermo Hollywood • 3964-5222 • www.rendezvoushotel. com.ar • $$$

4 Waldorf Hotel
A woody, light lobby sets a pleasing tone at Waldorf, which has appealing standard rooms with spotless en-suites and cable TV. Pricier superiors are contemporary with flat-screen TV and wooden flooring. 🕙 Map Q5 • Paraguay 450, Microcentro • 4312-2071 • www. waldorf-hotel.com.ar • $$

5 Hotel Bel Air
The fancy, white-washed façade of this elegant 1920s Recoleta building conceals 77 well-appointed, if a little dated in decor, rooms. Good amenities with restaurant, wine bar, mini-gym, business center, and baby-sitting service. 🕙 Map P5 • Arenales 1462, Recoleta • 4021-4000 • www. hahoteles.com • $$$$

6 Dazzler Suites Arroyo
This hotel is a short stroll from downtown. The interior needs a lick of paint, but suites are well equipped. Standard "classics" feature bedroom, lounge area, and kitchenette. There is a petite heated pool with sun deck, poolside breakfast bar, restaurant, gym, and sauna. 🕙 Map Q4 • Suipacha 1359, Retiro • 5276-7700 • www. arroyotowers.com • $$

7 Duque Hotel
This charming, award-winning hotel is well located within walking distance of the heart of Palermo Soho's trendy bars and restaurants. It offers the complete package, with a spa, a library, a cocktail bar, an outdoor pool, and even a barbecue. Rooms are big and the staff are friendly and helpful. 🕙 Map K3 • Guatemala 4364 • 4832-8189 • www.duquehotel. com • $$$

8 Carsson Hotel
The Carsson provides old-fashioned charm. The lobby has a marble floor, dripping chandeliers, and antique oil paintings. Rooms are tastefully decorated and well equipped. 🕙 Map Q5 • Viamonte 650, Microcentro • 4131-3800 • www. hotelcarsson.com.ar • $$

9 Hotel de los Dos Congresos
This hotel is excellent value for money. Half the rooms have views of the Congreso Nacional. The inviting standard rooms are bright and airy, but for just US$5 more, you get a spacious suite with sofa and Jacuzzi. 🕙 Map D1 • Rivadavia 1777, Congreso • 4372-0466 • www.hoteldoscongresos. com • $$$$$

10 Castelar Hotel and Spa
Opened in 1929 and once the favorite of aristocrats and writers, the Castelar is a throwback to Buenos Aires' golden age. Rooms today still ooze tradition and elegance. The best feature is the marbled spa with statued Turkish baths. 🕙 Map E2 • Avda. de Mayo 1152, Congreso • 4383-5000 • www.caste larhotel.com.ar • $$$

Left **Che Lulu Guest House** Right **Bonito San Telmo**

🔟 B&Bs & Guesthouses

1 1555 Malabia House

A beautifully restored convent, this B&B combines frescoes with contemporary furnishings. The soothing ambience is aided by indoor and outdoor patios. Amenities include gym, library, and executive lounge. 🗺 *Map K4 • Malabia 1555, Palermo Viejo • 4833-2410 • www.malabiahouse.com.ar • $$$*

2 Che Lulu Guest House

Hippy-chic guesthouse with eight rooms; two en-suite doubles. Choose between Mexican, minimalist, or "kitsch oriental pop art." The lounge features vintage furniture. A patio and terrace provide external space. 🗺 *Map K3 • Pasaje Emilio Zolá 5185, Palermo Viejo • 4772-0289 • www.chelulu.com • $$*

3 Cypress In

This modern B&B has 13 rooms, two with a street balcony. Doubles are on the small side, but brightly painted. Amenities include a lounge with leather sofas and DVD player, and a sun-kissed roof terrace. 🗺 *Map K3 • Costa Rica 4828, Palermo Viejo • 4833-5834 • www.cypressin.com • $$*

4 Abode Buenos Aires

Let an English breakfast kick-start the day, courtesy of Abode's British owners. The four rooms here are each prettily and individually furnished. 🗺 *Map J3 • Costa Rica 5193, Palermo Viejo • 15-3152-0170 • www.abodebuenosaires.com • $$$*

5 Posada Palermo

Architect Viviana converted her home, a traditional Palermo *casa chorizo* (sausage house), into this B&B. The result is four stylish rooms, furnished with recycled antiques. A patio and large living room complete a homey stay. Breakfasts are excellent, too. 🗺 *Map L4 • Salguero 1655, Palermo Viejo • 4826-8792 • www.posadapalermo.com.ar • $*

6 Lugar Gay de Buenos Aires

Buenos Aires' first gay B&B is housed in a restored, refurbished residence dating from 1900. There are eight modern, homely rooms, plus sauna, adult-video library, and exterior terraces. Helpful staff organize in-house tango classes and dinner parties as well as city tours. 🗺 *Map F3 • Defensa 1120, San Telmo • 4300-4747 • www.lugargay.com.ar • $$*

7 Pop Hotel

This hotel has popped up to give new meaning to the term "budget". Bright and breezy, with clean designs in each of the 44 rooms, this urban lodging doesn't cut corners, offering Wi-Fi, i-Pod docks, and a lounge. 🗺 *Map J4 • Juan Ramírez de Velasco 793, Villa Crespo • 4770-6900 • www.pophotelsbuenosaires.com • $$$*

8 Querido B&B

This cozy Anglo-Brazilian-run B&B is good value, with Egyptian cotton sheets, flatscreen TVs, and double glazing. It's modern, refreshing and welcoming, and has a relaxed atmosphere. 🗺 *Map J4 • Juan Ramírez de Velazco 934, Villa Crespo • 4854-6297 • www.queridobuenosaires.com • $$$*

9 Bonito San Telmo

This 1897 Bourgeois home has five sharply styled suites with soaring ceilings, spiral staircases, antique furniture, and a 19th-century piano. Enjoy the vast terrace space and sun-splashed rooftop gardens. 🗺 *Map F4 • Avda. Juan de Garay 458, San Telmo • 4362-8451 • www.bonitobuenosaires.com • $$$*

🔟 Posada de la Luna

A perfectly preserved 1860s house with bundles of colonial charm and shabby-chic decor. Apart from five rooms, it also has a lounge, a massage salon, Jacuzzi, and Andalusian patios. 🗺 *Map F2 • Perú 565, San Telmo • 4343-0911 • www.posadaluna.com • $$$$*

Room rates may vary with season, availability, specials, and promotions. All prices listed are high-season rates.

OSTINATTO
BUENOS AIRES HOSTEL

Price Categories

For a standard, double room per night (with breakfast if included), taxes, and extra charges.	**$** under US$50
	$$ US$50–110
	$$$ US$110–170
	$$$$ US$170–240
	$$$$$ over US$240

Ostinatto Buenos Aires Hostel sign

🔟 Budget Hotels & Hostels

1 Goya Hotel
The pick of downtown budget hotels, the Goya's best feature is its top floor featuring a terrace with city views, breakfast bar, and three suites. Lower floors have comfortable rooms with hydromassage baths. All have cable TV and are Wi-Fi or broadband enabled. ◈ Map Q5 • Suipacha 748, Microcentro • 4322-9269 • www.goyahotel.com.ar • $

2 Hostel Carlos de Gardel
This lively, friendly hostel, located in a historic house in San Telmo, has two air-conditioned dorms and eleven private rooms. Fully-equipped apartments are also available for rent. ◈ Map F3 • Carlos Calvo 579, San Telmo • 4307-2606 • www.hostelcarlosgardel.com • $

3 Hotel del Prado
A 1930s building entered via a marble stairway, the Prado is a good choice. Inviting, clean rooms have cable TV, ceiling fans, and are Wi-Fi-enabled; back rooms are quieter. Close to the subway and main bus routes. ◈ Map M5 • Paraguay 2385, Barrio Norte • 4961-1192 • www.hotedelprado-ba.com.ar • $$

4 Gran Hotel Hispano
This gem of a hotel is a Belle Époque building with two floors and an airy Spanish patio. Rooms are tasteful and clean. There is a garden terrace. ◈ Map E2 • Avda. de Mayo 861, Monserrat • 4345-2020 • www.hhispano.com.ar • $$

5 Hostel Inn Tango City
Set in an old San Telmo townhouse, this lively hostel has mixed and single-sex dorms, doubles, quadruples, plus book-exchange, laundry, and in-house travel agency. Best of all is a grungy basement bar with pool table, Internet, and very long happy hours. ◈ Map E3 • Piedras 680, San Telmo • 4300-5764 • www.hitangocity.com • $$

6 Ostinatto Buenos Aires Hostel
Ostinatto features a resto-bar, bijou wine cellar with own label, and free yoga and tango classes. The building's hamster-cage design links dorms, doubles with private bathroom, loft apartment, and communal roof-terrace with criss-crossing walkways. Lockers and laundry service are provided. ◈ Map F3 • Chile 680, San Telmo • 4362-9639 • www.ostinatto.com • $

7 Back in BA Hostel
Located in Palermo Viejo, Back in BA is a friendly hostel close to all the action. The room rate includes linen, breakfast, Wi-Fi, tea, and coffee, making it a popular choice. There's also a bar that is open till late, a kitchen, and cable TV. ◈ Map J3 • El Salvador 5115, Palermo Viejo • 4774-2859 • www.backinba.com • $

8 Palermo Soho Hostel
Located in Palermo's trendy shopping zone, this hostel has more doubles than dorms, making it ideal for the backpacking couple. Chill-out spaces include a terrace, a lounge, and a pleasant balcony. ◈ Map J2 • Nicaragua 4728 • 4833-0151 • www.palermosohohostel.com.ar • $

9 Milhouse
This is the city's party hostel. Activities include nightly drinking games, pool tournaments, and nightclub visits. It has a patio and roof-terrace. ◈ Map E2 • Hipólito Yrigoyen 959, Monserrat • 4345-9604 • www.milhousehostel.com • $

10 V&S Hostel
Occupying a beautiful 1910 building with winding stairway and an antique elevator, V&S is a calm oasis amidst the madness of downtown. There are dorms, doubles, quadruples, a patio, a lounge, and a small library. Spanish and tango classes are available. ◈ Map Q5 • Viamonte 887, Microcentro • 4322-0994 • www.hostelclub.com • $

Most of the budget hotels and hostels do not have air-conditioning, disabled access, or accept credit cards.

General Index

1555 Malabia House 116
562 Nogaró Buenos Aires 113
725 Continental Hotel 112
878 92

A

Adobe Buenos Aires 116
ATMs 108
A.Y. Not Dead 90
Abasto 64
Abraxas 110
Acabar 89, 92
accommodations
  B&Bs and guesthouses 116
  boutique hotels 114
  budget hotels and hostels 117
  high-end and business hotels 113
  luxury hotels 112
  mid-range hotels 115
  tips 111
activities for children 60–61
  children's shops 61
  traveling with kids 111
Aerolíneas Argentinas 104
Aeroparque Jorge Newbury 96
Ain, Casimiro 28
Air France 104
airlines 104
airports 104
Aldo's Vinoteca 77
Alitalia 104
alfajores 53
Alto Palermo 39
Alvear Palace Hotel 112
American 104
La Americana 57, 67
Amerika 48
Amici Miei 77
Antigua Tasca de Cuchilleros 77
Antiguas, Adolfo Martinez Armas 84
Antigüedades Antigüa 84
antiques 110
Apertura de la Ópera 42
  see also festivals
Attaque 77 59
architecture 34–5
Armada 43
Art Hotel 114

Arte BA 35, 88
Arte de Mafia 91
Artistas Jóvenes Argentinos 84
ASATEJ 102
Asociación Mutua Israelita Argentina 33, 58
Ateneo Grand Splendid 110
Automóvil Club Argentina 35
Autoria 84
Avenida 9 de Julio 6, 14, **20–21**, 65, 81
Avenida Corrientes 66, 69
Avenida de Mayo 6, **14–15**, 64–5, 67
Avis 104
Axel Hotel 112
Azema Exotic Bistró 93

B

B&Bs and guesthouses 116
BA Fashion Week 35, 88
Baar Fun Fun 97, 99
Back in BA 117
Banco de la Nación 9
Banco Hipotecario Nacional 34
banking 108
bars and cafés
  Barrio Norte, Recoleta & Around 70
  Microcentro, Puerto Madero & Retiro 85
  outside Buenos Aires 99
  Palermo 92
  San Telmo 77
Bar 6 57, 92
Bar Britanico 57
Bar Celta 70
Bar El Federal 57
Bar La Paz 69
Bar Plaza Dorrego 18, 57, 70, 75, 77
Bar Sur 75, 77
La Barra 98
Barrio Histórico, Colonia 98
Barrio Norte 64
Barrio Norte, Recoleta & Around 64–9
  bars and cafés 70
  Recoleta stores 68
  restaurants 71
Basílica Nuestra Señora de la Merced 82

Benediction Chapel 10
Benedit Bis 68
Bengal 85
Berni, Antonio 17, 23
Bersuit Vergabarat 59
Biblioteca Nacional 34
La Biela 10, 67, 70
Big One 49
Bigatti, Alfredo 40
biking 105
Bike Tours 105
Bio 93
Blaqué 84
La Boca 26, 72 see also San Telmo and La Boca
Boca Juniors 73–4
La Bombonera 73, 75
Bombonella 69
Bonita San Telmo 116
book stores 110
Borges, Jorge Luis 33, 59, 81, 85
Botero, Fernando 23
Botica del Angel 27
La Bourgogne 57, 71
boutique hotels 114
El Boyero 38
Brasserie Petanque 56, 77
La Brigada 54
British Airways 104
Brown, William 11
Brujas 91
budget hotels 117
budget tips 107
Buenos Aires Design 39
Buenos Aires Fashion Week 42
Buller Brewing Company 70
Buquebus 25, 95
buses 104–5
  local 104
  long-distance shuttle 104
business hotels 113
Bustillo, Alejandro 35

C

Cabaña Las Lilas 85
El Cabildo 8, 42, 83
La Cabrera 54, 93
cabs see taxis
Cadore 69
Caesar Park 112
cafés see bars and cafés
Café de los Angelitos 45
Café Iberia 14

Café La Puerto Rico 8
Café Los 36 Billares 15
Café Tortoni 15, 26, 57
Caix 47
Calamaro, Andrés 59
Calle Arroyo 20
Calle de los Suspiros
 Colonia 25
La Calle de los Títeres 60
Calle Florida 81, 83
Calle Lavalle 21
El Callejón 97
El Caminito 73, 75
Campo Argentino de Polo
 88
Campo dei Fiori 71
Canal 7 35
La Cancha 77
Cantina Pierino 71
Capital Diseño y Objetos
 90
car rental 104
Carla Di Sí 90
Carnal 91
Carnaval 42 see also
 festivals
Carsson Hotel 115
Casa Brandon 49
Casa Cruz 57, 93
Casa de la Cultura 15
La Casa de las Botas 90
Casa Las Cañitas 114
Casa López 38
Casa Mínima 73, 75
Casa Nacarello, Colonia 25
Casa Rosada 8, 15, 65
Casa Saltshaker 71
Casares, Adolfo Bioy 33
Casino Central 98
Castelar Hotel & Spa 115
La Catedral 45
Catedral Metropolitana 8,
 83
La Cayetana Historic
 House 114
Celedonio 68
cell phones 108 see also
 phone rental
Cementerio de la Recoleta
 6, 10–11, 37, 65, 67
Cementerio la Chacarita 27
Centro Cultural Borges 81
Centro Cultural Recoleta
 66, 69
Centro Cultural Torquato
 Tasso 44
Che Lulu Guest House 116
Chez Nous 56

Chemical Brothers 46
children's shops 61
Chiquilín 55
Chiquín 27
La Cholita 54
churches
 Basílica Nuestra Señora
  de la Merced 82
 Benediction Chapel 10
 Catedral Metropolitana
  8, 83
 Iglesia Matriz, Colonia
  25
 Iglesia Nuestra Señora
  de Belén 19
 Iglesia Ortodoxa Rusa 74
El Centinela 95, 98
La Cigale 85
cinema 43
City Gate, Colonia 25
Claridge 113
Clásica y Moderna 57, 70
clubs see nightclubs
El Club 99
Club 69 46, 48
Club Aráoz 47
Club Boutique 46
Colonia del Sacramento,
 Uruguay 7, 24–5, 95
 Barrio Histórico 98
 Calle de los Suspiros 25
 Casa Nacarello 25
 El Faro and Convento de
  San Francisco 24
 Iglesia Matriz 25
 Museo Portugués 24
 Playa Ferrando 25
 Plaza Mayor 24
 El Portón de Campo 25
 Rambla Costanera 25
 Real de San Carlos 25
Comedor Nikkai 77
Comme il Faut 27
communications 108
Confitería Colón 57
Confitería El Molino 34
Confitería Ideal 26
consulates 109
Copes, Juan Carlos 28
Correo Argentino 108
Correo Central 69
Cortázar, Julio 33
craft stores 38–9
Creamfields 43
credit cards 108
crime 106 see also theft
 prevention
Crobar 47

Crónica Bar 92
La Cuadrada 99
Cualquier Verdura 76
El Cuartito 71
cultural events 107
Cumaná 71
La Cupertina 93
currency 103 see also
 money
custom limits 103
cycling see biking
Cypress In 116

D
Dadá 85
Dazzler Suites Arroyo 115
Dazzler Tower 113
The December Riots 33
Deira, Ernesto 23
De Maria 68
dental treatment 109
Design Suites 113
El Desnivel 54
Dill & Drinks 85
dining 111
Dirección Nacional de
 Migraciones 103
disabled travelers 102
 transport 105
Disquería Bird 110
La Dorita 55
Dorrego-Ortíz Basualdo 11
driving 103
 car rental 104
 driver's license 103
 rush hour 106
El Drugstore 24, 99
Duhau Restaurante 56, 71
dulche de leche 52
Duque 115

E
Edificio Drabble 15
Edificio la Inmobiliaria 14
El Faro and Convento de
 San Francisco Colonia
 24
electricity 103
emergency numbers 109
empanadas 52
Escarlata 91
Espacio Ecléctico 76
Esplendor de Buenos
 Aires 114
Estación Constitutión 21
Estación Sur 39
Estatua del Quijote 21
Eterna Cadencia 91

Eternautas 10, 105
Ex-Ministry of Public
  Works 21

F
Faena Hotel and Universe
  112
Falklands War 33, 36, 81
Farmacia de la Estrella 66
fax 108
Felix 90
La Feria 98
Feria Internacional del
  Libro de Buenos Aires
  42, 88
Ferrer, Horacio 28
ferries 104
Festival Buenos Aires
  Tango 42
Festival Internacional de
  Cine Independiente 42
festivals 42–3
Fierro 114
FILO 83, 85
La Feria de Mataderos 98
Flavio Serrati Arte y
  Antigüedades 76
Floralis Genérica 35
Florida Garden 85
food 52–3
  cheap eats 107
  parrillas 54–5
  restaurants 56–7
Forner, Raquel 40
Four Seasons Hotel 21, 112
Frank's 92
French Embassy 20
fugazzetta rellena 53
Fundación Forner-Bigatti 40
Fundación Proa 73, 75

G
Galería 5ta Avenida 39
Galería Bond Street 39
Galería Güemes 39, 83
Galerías Pacífico 39, 81
galleries 76
Gandhi Galerna 69
García, Charly 58
Gardel, Carlos 27, **28–9**,
  32, 45, 58, 64, 67
gay and lesbian travelers
  102
  Axel Hotel 112
  gay clubs and hangouts
  48–9
  Lugar Gay de Buenos
  Aires 116

gay and lesbian travelers
  (cont.)
  Marcha del Orgullo Gay
  43
  Pride Travel 103
Gibraltar 77
Gil Antigüedades 76
Gimenez, Susana 58
GLAM 48
The Gotan Project 29
Gout Café 49
Goya Hotel 117
Goya y Lucientes,
  Francisco José de 16
Gran Bar Danzón 70
Gran Hotel Hispano 117
Gran Parilla del Plata 55
Groove 43
guesthouses 116
Guevara Art Gallery 76
guided tours 105

H
HB Antigüedades 76
health 103, 109
Hermanos Estebecorena
  90
Hernández, José 33, 87
Hertz 104
HG Restaurant 93
high-end hotels 113
Hilton Buenos Aires 113
history 32–3
Home Hotel Buenos
  Aires 114
hospitals 109
hostels 117
Hostel Carlos de Gardel
  117
Hostel Inn Tango City 117
Hotel Bel Air 115
Hotel del Prado 117
Hotel Castelar 15
Hotel Chile 14, 67
Hotel Colón 115
Hotel de los Congresos 115
Hotel Emperador 113
Hotel Madero 112
Humawaca 90

I
Iberia 104
Iglesia Matriz, Colonia 25
Iglesia Nuestra Señora de
  Belén 19
Iglesia Ortodoxa Rusa 74
Intercontinental Buenos
  Aires 113

internet 108
Isla Martín García 97
  Presidential residences
  98
Israeli Embassy 33, 83

J
Jack The Ripper (bar) 70
Jardín Botánico Carlos
  Thays 36
Jardín Japonés 87, 89
Jardín Oculto 76
Jardín Zoológico 61, 89
Joyería Isaac Katz 39
Joyería Paula Levy/Viviana
  Carriquiry 38

K
The Kavanagh 14, 34
Kelly's 38
KEY 97
Kika 47
KMØ 48
Kosiuko 68
Krista Hotel Boutique 114
Kuitca, Guillermo 23

L
L'Ago 76
launderettes 107
leather goods 110
Lezama 77
Library, Teatro Colón 13
Ligier 110
El Living 47
Lo de Charlie 99
locro 53
Los Fabulosos Cadillacs 59
Lufthansa 104
Lulu of London 68
Lugar Gay de Buenos
  Aires 116
luxury hotels 112

M
Las Madres de la Plaza de
  Mayo 9, 59
magazines 102
Magdalena's Party 92
mail 108
Maizani, Azucena 28
Maldita Milonga 45
Mandarine 46
Manes, Pablo Curatella 22
Mansión Alzaga Unzué 21
Mansión Dandi Royal 27,
  114
Manuel Tienda León 104

Manzana de las Luces 67
Mar del Plata 95
  Casino Central 98
  Playa Bristol 95
Maradona, Diego 33, 58, 73, 74
Marcha de Orgullo Gay 43
María Cher 90
María Vásquez 68
Marriot Plaza Hotel 112
Masottatorres 76
Mataderos 97
Martínez, Tomás Eloy 33
mate 38, 53
Martín, José de San 32, 81
May Revolution 32, 40, 42
medical clinics see hospitals
Meliá Recoleta Plaza 114
Menem, Carlos 58
Mendoza, Pedro de 32
Mercado del San Telmo 75
Mesón de la Plaza, El 99
Mi Vaca y Yo 99
Microcentro 80
Microcentro, Puerto Madero & Retiro 80–83
  bars 85
  restaurants 85
  stores 84
mid-range hotels 115
Milhouse 117
Milión 70
Millai Sumaj 84
milongas see tango clubs and milongas
Ministerio de Economía 9
Míro, Joan 65, 81
Mission 38
Mitre, Bartólome 37, 82
mobile phones see cell phones
Modena Design 16
Molina, Juana 59
money 103
  bank transfers 108
  currency 103
  currency exchange 108
  traveler's checks 108
Monserrat 64
Montevideo 95, 98
  Ciudad Vieja 95, 98
  Plaza Independencia 95, 98
Monument to General Manuel Belgrano 9, 82
Moreno 376 114
Mundo Bizarro 92

Museo Argentino de Ciencias Naturales 60
Museo Argentino del Títere 60
Museo Casa Carlos Gardel 67
Museo Casa de Ricardo Rojas 40
Museo de Arte Hispanoamericano Isaac Fernández Blanco 21
Museo de Arte Latinoamericano de Buenos Aires (MALBA) 7, 22–3, 87, 89
Museo de Artes Plásticas Eduardo Sívori 41
Museo de Arte Popular José Hernández 21, 33, 87
Museo de Arte Tigre 98
Museo de la Ciudad 66
Museo de la Deuda Externa 41
Museo de la Pasión Boquense 74
Museo de los Niños 61
Museo del Cine 41
Museo Evita 87, 89
Museo Fortabat 40
Museo Fragata Sarmiento 41
Museo Histórico de Cera 40
Museo Historico Nacional 74 see also Parque Lezama
Museo de la Inmigración 40
Museo Mitre 37, 82
Museo Nacional de Bellas Artes 6, 16–17, 65
Museo Portugués, Colonia 24
Museo Xul Solar 88
museums 40–41
  Botica del Angel 27
  Fundación Forner-Bigatti 40
  Museo Argentino de Ciencias Naturales 60
  Museo Argentino del Títere 60
  Museo Casa Carlos Gardel 67
  Museo Casa de Ricardo Rojas 40

museums (cont.)
  Museo de Arte Hispanoamericano Isaac Fernández Blanco 21
  Museo de Arte Latinoamericano de Buenos Aires (MALBA) 7, 22–3, 87, 89
  Museo de Arte Popular José Hernández 21, 33, 87
  Museo de Artes Plásticas Eduardo Sívori 41
  Museo de Arte Tigre 98
  Museo de la Ciudad 66
  Museo de la Deuda Externa 41
  Museo de la Pasión Boquense 74
  Museo de la Policia Federal de Argentina 40
  Museo de los Niños 61
  Museo del Cine 41
  Museo Evita 87, 89
  Museo Fortabat 40
  Museo Fragata Sarmiento 41
  Museo Histórico de Cera 40
  Museo Historico Nacional 74 see also Parque Lezama
  Museo Mitre 37, 82
  Museo Nacional de Bellas Artes 6, 16–17, 65
  Museo Portugués, Colonia 24
  Museo Xul Solar 88
  Palacio de las Aguas Corrientes 34
  El Zanjón 41, 75
music 110
Musimundo 111

N
La Nación 37
La Nacional 26
Nacional Congreso 14
Nectarine 2.0 57, 71
newspapers 102
NH City and Tower 113
nightclubs 46–7
Nino Bien 44
noche de los museos (gallery nights) 107
Notorious 70

Index

Nuevo Salón la Argentina 45

O
El Obelisco 20, 81, 83
El Obrero 54
Ocampo, Victoria 33
Olsen 56, 93
Ona Sáez 68
Once 64
Opción Sur 105
Ostinatto Buenos Aires Hostel 117
Oui Oui 56
outside Buenos Aires 94–8
    bars 99
    restaurants 99
Oxiro 91

P
Pabellón 4, 91
Pachá 46
Páez, Fito 59
Palacio Barolo 14, 34, 67
Palacio de Justicia 36
Palacio de las Aguas Corrientes 34
Palacio del Congreso 65
Palacio Vera 15
Palermo 86–9, 91
    bars 92
    restaurants 93
    shopping 90
Palermo Chico 86
Palermo Viejo 86
Pampa Picante 91
Palermo Soho Hostel 117
Pantheon of Outstanding Citizens 11
Paraje Arevalo 93
Parrillada 52
parrillas (steakhouses) 54–5
Park Hyatt Buenos Aires 112
parks and gardens see plazas and green spaces
Parque 3 de Febrero 61, 106
Parque de la Costa 61
Parque Las Heras 37
Parque Lezama 74
Parque Rodo 97
Parrilla Lezama 75
Paseo Alcorta 39
La Pasionaria 90
passports 103
Patagonia Sur 56, 77
El Patio 85

Patio Bullrich 39
Paz, José C. 11, 65
Pellegrini, Carlos 11, 37
Perón, Eva Maria Duarte de 32, 58, 65, 87
    family vault 10
Perón, Juan Domingo 28, 32, 58
Pestana Buenos Aires 113
Petite Colón Confitería 12, 21, 57
phone rental 108
Piazzolla, Astor 28, 44
Piazzolla Tango 27
picnics 107
Pilar Church 11
Pinamar 96, 98
Pirámide de Mayo 9
El Planetario Galileo Galilei 60, 89
Plata Lappas 38
Plata Nativa 84
Playa Ferrando Colonia 25
plazas and green spaces 36–7
    Jardín Japonés 87, 89
    Parque 3 de Febrero 61, 106
    Parque de la Costa 61
    Parque Las Heras 37
    Parque Lezama 74
    Parque Rodo 97
    Plaza de los Dos Congresos 14
    Plaza de Mayo 6, **8–9**, 32, 64, 67, 81, 83
    Plaza Dorrego 74
    Plaza Embajada de Israel 33, 83
    Plaza Francia 37
    Plaza Independencia 98
    Plaza Julio Cortazar 37–8, 89
    Plaza Lavalle 36
    Plaza Mayor Colonia 24
    Plaza Mitre 37
    Plaza Rodríguez Peña 36
    Plaza San Martín 36, 81, 83
    Plaza Serrano see Plaza Julio Cortazar
    Plaza Vicente López 36
    Plazoleta Carlos Pellegrini 37
    Plazoleta Cataluña 21
Podestá Super Club de Copas 46
police 109

polo 88
Polo Club 84
Pop Hotel 116
El Portón de Campo, Colonia 25
Posada de la Luna 116
La Prensa 11
Presidential residences 98
Pride Café 49, 57
Pride Travel 102
provoleta 52
public holidays 102
Puente de la Mujer 82
Puente Nicolas Avellaneda 75
Puente Transbordador 74
Puerto Madero 24, 40, 58, 80
Pugliese, Osvaldo 28
Puig, Manuel 33
Punta del Este 96
Puro Diseño 68

Q
El Querandí 44
Querido B&B 116
Quilmes Rock Festival 42
    see also festivals
Quirós, Cesáreo Bernaldo de 17
QRV – Transportes Especiales 105

R
Rambla Costanera, Colonia 25
Ramos Generales 39
Real de San Carlos, Colonia 25
Recoleta 64, 68
Recoleta Monastry 66
Rembrandt 16
remis (mini-cab) 104–5
Rendez-Vous 115
La Renga 59
República de Acá 91
Reserva Ecológica Costanera Sur 82–3
restaurants 56–7
    Barrio Norte, Recoleta & Around 71
    dining tips 111
    Microcentro, Puerto Madero & Retiro 85
    outside Buenos Aires 99
    Palermo 93
    San Telmo 77

Restó 71
Retiro 65, 80
Rey, Patricio 59
Rigoletto Curioso 69
Río de la Plata 24
River Delta boat rides 60
Rivera, Diego 73
The Roxy 46
Rúa de la, Fernando 33
Rubens 16
La Rural 35
rush hour 106

S
Sabater Hnos. Fabrica de
   Jabones 90
Sábato, Ernesto 33
sales taxes 110
Salón Canning 45
San Antonio de Areco 96
   Centro Historico 98
   Día de la Tradición 96
   Plaza Ruiz de Arellano 96
San Telmo 7, **18–19**, 41,
   44, 70, 72
San Telmo and La Boca
   72–5
   bars 77
   galleries 76
   restaurants 77
   shopping 76
Santaolalla, Gustavo 59
Sarmiento, Domingo
   Faustino 10, 33, 41
Saura, Carlos 29
Se Dice de Mí 84
security 109
   theft prevention 109
Seguí, Antonio 17, 23
The Shamrock 70
Sheraton Buenos Aires
   Hotel and Convention
   Center 113
shopping 110
   book stores 110
   children's shops 61
   craft stores 38–9
   Microcentro, Puerto
   Madero & Retiro 84
   Mercado de las Pulgas
   110
   Palermo 90
   Recoleta 68
   San Telmo 76
   shopping centers 39
   Sunday Antiques Market
   18, 74, 110
   tips 110

Silvia Petroccia 76
Sin Rumbo 45
Sipan 85
Sitges 48
soccer 33, 40, 47, 58,73–4
   World Cup victory 33
Soda Stereo 59
Sofitel Buenos Aires 112
Solar, Xul 19, 22
Solo Tango 27
sorrentinos 52
Soul Café 92
souvenirs 110
Spell Café 91
Status 71
steakhouses *see parrillas*
student travelers 102
subway 105
Sugar 92
Sunday Antiques Market
   18, 74, 110

T
Tandil 95
tango 7, **26–7**, 32, 42, 64
   Festival Buenos Aires
   Tango 42
   tango artists 28–9
   Tango Brujo 84
   tango clubs and
   milongas 44–5
Tangol 105
Tanguería El Beso 44
Tante 99
taxes and refunds 110
taxis 104–5, 106, 109
   radio taxis 104
   remise 104–5
Teatro Avenida 15
Teatro Colón 6, **12–13**, 20,
   36, 42, 66
Teatro Gran Rex 69
Teatro Metropolitan 69
Teatro San Martín 69
telephone 108
   phone rentals 108
Templo Libertad 36
La Terraza 99
Terroir 110
theft prevention 109
Tiempo de Gitanos Bar y
   Fonda 92
Tigre 61, 96
time zone 103
Timerman, Jacobo 33
Tomo 1 57, 85
Torcuato de Alvear 15,
   58–9

tourist information desks
   102
trains 105
trams 105
Tramando 68
transport 104–5
El Trapiche 54, 93
travelers
   disabled travelers 102
   gay and lesbian travelers
   102
   student travelers 102
   women travelers 109
traveler's checks 108
traveling with kids 111
Tren de la Costa 60, 96
Troilo, Aníbal 28
El Túnel 15

U
Ulises 115
United 104

V
Varela, Adriana 44
Vasalissa 68
El Ventanal 15
Vicente 99
Videla, Jorge Rafael 59
El Viejo Almacén 44
Vinos & Bodegas 35
visas 103
La Vitrina 39
V&S Hostel 117

W
Waldorf Hotel 115
walking 105
Walrus Books 110
water 109
weather 103, 106
Western Union 108
Wine 53
Winery 20
women travelers 109
World Cup victory 33

Z
El Zanjón 41, 75
Zavdarie Doc 93
Zival's 27
ZOOM 48
Zum Edelweiss 69

Acknowledgments

The Authors
Declan McGarvey visited Argentina in 1999 and decided to stay after falling in love with the country. Nine presidents later, he remains in Buenos Aires, where he works as a travel writer and editor. He contributed to the *Eyewitness Guide to Argentina*, has collaborated on and edited several Time Out guides to Patagonia and Buenos Aires, and has contributed to DK's *Where to Go When* series.

Jonathan Schultz previously co-authored DK titles *Eyewitness Top 10 Boston* and *RealCity* New York. His love for Buenos Aires, first kindled on a college exchange program, was reignited after an eight-year absence, compelling him to pick up roots and live there again in 2007. *Dulce de leche* and *asados* feature weekly in his porteño diet.

Publisher
Douglas Amrine

List Manager
Christine Stroyan

Managing Art Editor
Mabel Chan

Senior Editor
Sadie Smith

Senior Designer
Paul Jackson

Senior Cartographic Editor
Casper Morris

DTP Operator
Natasha Lu

Production Controller
Louise Minihane

Photographer
Demetrio Carrasco

Additional Photography
Rough Guides/Greg Roden

Fact Checker
Ariel Waisman

Senior Cartographer
Suresh Kumar

Cartographer
Schchida Nand Pradhan

Revisions Team
Claire Baranowski, Emer FitzGerald, Lydia Halliday, Nicola Malone, Margaret McHugh, Sorrel Moseley-Williams, Rada Radojicic, Marisa Renzullo, Ellen Root, Susana Smith

Declan McGarvey would like to thank Colin Barraclough, Lucas at Eternautas, and most of all Virginia Maccallini for their invaluable help during the writing of this book. He would also like to say a huge thank you to Sadie Smith at DK London and the staff at Quadrum Solutions, Mumbai, India for their unflagging support and patience.

Picture Credits
Key: a-above; b-below/bottom; c-centre; f-far; l-left; r-right; t-top.

Works of art have been reproduced with the kind permission of the following copyright holders: *Manifestacion* (1934) Antonio Berni, Courtesy of Jose Berni 23cb; *Siste últimas canciones* (1986) Guillermo Kuitca, Courtesy of Sperone Westwater Art Gallery, New York 23cr; *The Butcher and Don Juan Sandoval, the Boss* Cesáreo Bernaldo de Quirós, in cooperation with the artist's grandson, Mario C. Bernaldo de Quirós 17cr; *Pareja* (1923) Xul Solar, reserved rights by Foundation Pan Klub – Xul Solar Museum 22bc ; *Drago* Xul Solar, reserved rights by Foundation Pan Klub – Xul Solar Museum 89tl.

The Publisher would like to thank the following individuals, companies and picture libraries for their kind permissions to reproduce their photographs:

Courtesy of ACABAR: 92tr.

ALAMY IMAGES: APEIRON-PHOTO 29cr; Nick Baylis 42tl; Javier Etcheverry 97tl; Evernight Images 42tr; David R Frazier Photolibrary, Inc 12cl; Bernardo Galmarini 14cl, 50–51; Jeremy Hoare 6crb, 12–13c, 13tr, 20br, 42b; North River Images 4–5; Pictorial Press Ltd 58tl; Christopher Pillitz 58b, 59tl; Guido Schiefer 28tr; vario images GmbH & Co.KG 58tr; wim wiskerke 35tr; Yadid Levy 20–21c, 78–9.

LA CABRERA: 54tl; CORBIS: Bettmann 32tl; Pablo Corral V 12bc, 13bc; Stevens Frémont 114tl; Jon Hicks 24-5c; FIERRO HOTEL: 93tl; LANGEVIN JACQUES 28b; Sergio Pitamitz 3br, 62–3; Hubert Stadler 64tr. FOTOSCOPIO LATIN AMERICA STOCK PHOTO AGENCY: 26cb, 48tr, 49tr.

LATINPHOTO: 43tl, 10–11c. MALBA – FUNDACION CONSTANTINI, BUENOS AIRES, ARGENTINA: 22bc, 22cl, 23cr, 23cb.

PETER & JACKIE MAIN: 13tl.

ODYSSEY PRODUCTIONS, INC: Robert Frerck 13clb.

PHOTOLIBRARY: Japan Travel Bureau 95t; Nordic Photos/Chad Ehlers 8–9c.

REUTERS (alt TYPE): Marcos Haupa 32tr.

VISAGE: Robert Frerck 18–19c; Getty Images 28tl, 32bl, 33tl.

Special Editions of DK Travel Guides

Phrase Book

The variant of Spanish spoken in Argentina is known as rioplatense. "Ll" and "y" are both pronounced like the English "sh" as in "she." The "s" sound can become like an "h" when it occurs before another consonant or at the end of a word as in "tres" – "treh"; it may be omitted altogether, as in "dos" – "do". As in other Latin American countries, "c" and "z" are pronounced as "s" before "e" or "i" and as "k" otherwise.

In an Emergency

Help!	**¡Socorro!**	sokorro
Stop!	**¡Pare!**	pareh
Call a doctor!	**¡Llame a un médico!**	shame a oon medeeko
Call an ambulance	**¡Llame a una ambulancia**	shame a oona amboolans-ya
Police!	**¡Policía!**	poleesee-a
Where is the nearest hospital?	**¿Dónde queda el hospital más cercano?**	dondeh keda el ospeetal mas sairkano
Could you help me?	**¿Me puede ayudar?**	meh pwedeh a-shoodar

Communication Essentials

Yes	**Sí**	see
No	**No**	no
Please	**Por favor**	por fabor
Pardon me	**Perdone**	pairdoneh
Excuse me	**Disculpe**	deeskoolpeh
I'm sorry	**Lo siento**	lo s-yento
Thanks	**Gracias**	gras-yas
Hello!	**¡hola!**	olah
Good day	**Buenos días**	bwenos dee-as
Good afternoon	**Buenas tardes**	bwenas tardes
Good evening	**Buenas noches**	bwenas noches
Night	**Noche**	nocheh
Morning	**Mañana**	man-yana
Tomorrow	**Mañana**	man-yana
Yesterday	**Ayer**	a-shair
Here	**Acá**	aka
How?	**¿Cómo?**	komo
When?	**¿Cuándo?**	kwando
Where?	**¿Dónde?**	dondeh
Why?	**¿Por qué?**	por keh
Fine!	**¡Qué bien!**	keh b-yen

Useful Phrases

How are you?	**¿Qué tal?/ ¿Cómo va?**	keh tal/komo ba
Pleased to meet you	**Encantado/ mucho gusto**	enkantado/ moocho goosto
Do you speak a little English?	**¿Habla un poco de inglés?**	abla oon poko deh eengles
I don't understand	**No entiendo**	no ent-yendo
Could you speak more slowly?	**¿Puede hablar más despacio?**	pwedeh ablar mas despas-yo
How do I get to/ which way to..?	**¿Cómo se llega a...?/¿Por dónde se va a...?**	komo se shega a/ por dondeh seh ba a

Useful Words

large	**grande**	grandeh
small	**pequeño**	peken-yo
good	**bueno**	bweno
bad	**malo**	malo
open	**abierto**	ab-yairto
closed	**cerrado**	serrado

entrance	**entrada**	entrada
exit	**salida**	saleeda
right	**derecha**	dairecha
left	**izquierda**	eesk-yairda
straight on	**derecho**	dare-aich-oh
quickly	**pronto**	pronto
bathroom	**baño**	ban-yo
women	**mujeres**	moohaires
men	**hombres**	ombres
toilet paper	**papel higiénico**	papel eeh-yeneeko
batteries	**pilas**	peelas
passport	**pasaporte**	pasaporteh
visa	**visa**	beesa
tourist card	**tarjeta turística**	tarheta tooreesteeka
bar	**boliche**	boleecheh
money	**guita**	geeta
to eat	**comer**	com-air
driver's license	**registro**	reheestro

Health

I don't feel well	**Me siento mal**	meh s-yento mal
I have a stomach ache	**Me duele el estómago**	meh dweleh el estomago
headache	**la cabeza**	la kabesa
He/she is ill	**Está enfermo/a**	esta enfairmo/a
I need to rest	**Necesito descansar**	neseseeto deskansar

Post Offices and Banks

I'm looking for a Bureau de change	**Busco una casa de cambio**	boosko oona kasa deh kamb-yo
What is the dollar rate?	**¿Cuanto está el dolar?**	koo-an-toh esta el dolar
I want to send a letter	**Quiero enviar una carta**	k-yairo emb-yar oona karta
stamp	**sello**	se-jo
to draw out money	**sacar dinero**	sakar deenairo

Shopping

I would like/ want...	**Me gustaría/ quiero...**	meh goostaree-a/k-yairo
Do you have any...?	**¿Tiene...?**	t-yeneh
expensive	**caro**	karo
How much is it?	**¿Cuánto cuesta?**	kwanto kwesta
What time do you open/close?	**¿A qué hora abre/ cierra?**	a ke ora abreh/ s-yairra
May I pay with a credit card?	**¿Puedo pagar con tarjeta de crédito?**	pwedo pagar kon tarheta deh kredeeto

Sightseeing

road	**carretera**	karretaira
street	**calle, callejón**	ka-sheh, ka-shehon
tourist bureau	**oficina de turismo**	ofeeseena deh tooreesmo
town hall	**municipalidad**	mooneesee-paleedad

Getting Around

When does it leave?	**¿A qué hora sale?**	a keh ora saleh
When does the next train/bus leave for...?	**¿A qué hora sale el próximo tren/ autobús a...?**	a keh ora saleh el prokseemo tren/owtoboos a

customs	**aduana**	*adwana*
Could you call a taxi for me?	**¿Me puede llamar un taxi?**	*meh pwedeh shamar oon taksee*
port of embarkation	**puerta de embarque**	*pwairta deh embarkeh*
boarding pass	**tarjeta de embarque**	*tarheta deh embarkeh*
car hire	**alquiler de autos**	*alkeelair deh owtos*
bicycle	**bicicleta**	*beeseekleta*
rate	**tarifa**	*tareefa*
insurance	**seguro**	*segooro*
petrol station	**estación de nafta**	*estas-yon deh nafta*
I have a flat tyre	**Se me pinchó una goma**	*seh meh pin-choh oona goma*

Staying in a Hotel

I have a reservation	**Tengo una reserva**	*engo oona rresairba*
Are there any rooms available?	**¿Tiene habitaciones disponibles?**	*yones deesponeebles disponibles?*
single/double room	**habitación sencilla/doble**	*abeetas-yon sensee-sha/dobleh*
twin room	**habitación con camas simples**	*abeetas-yon kon kamas sim-plays*
shower	**ducha**	*doocha*
bath	**bañadera**	*ban-yadaira*
I want to be woken up at…	**Necesito que me despierten a las…**	*neseseeto keh meh desp-yairten a las*
water	**fría**	
soap	**jabón**	*habon*
towel	**toalla**	*to-a-sha*
key	**llave**	*shabeh*

Eating Out

I am a vegetarian	**Soy vegetariano**	*soy behetar-yano*
fixed price	**precio fijo**	*pres-yo feeho*
glass	**vaso**	*baso*
cutlery	**cubiertos**	*koob-yairtos*
Can I see the menu, please?	**¿Me deja ver el menú, por favor?**	*me deha ber el menoo por fabor*
The bill, please	**la cuenta, por favor**	*la kwenta por fabor*
I would like some water	**Quiero un poco de agua**	*k-yairo oon poko deh agwa*
breakfast	**desayuno**	*desa-shoono*
lunch	**almuerzo**	*almwairso*
dinner	**comida**	*komeeda*

Menu Decoder

bife de chorizo a caballo	*beefeh deh choreeso a kabasho*	char-grilled sirloin steak with two fried eggs on top
choripán	*choreepan*	pork sausage sandwich
churrasco a caballo	*choorrasko a kabasho*	char-grilled rump steak with two fried eggs on top
torta de humita	*torta deh oomeeta*	yellow sweet pumpkin and sweet corn mixed with cheese, onion, and red pepper

chimichurri	*cheemeechoorree*	hot sauce
centolla	*sentosha*	spider crab
bife de lomo	*beefeh deh lomo*	char-grilled fillet steak
mollejas	*moshehas*	sweetbreads
arroz	*arros*	rice
atún	*atoon*	tuna
azúcar	*asookar*	sugar
bacalao	*bakala-o*	cod
camarones	*kamarones*	prawns
carne	*karneh*	meat
chip	*cheep*	bread roll
huevo	*webo*	egg
jugo	*hoogo*	fruit juice
langosta	*langosta*	lobster
leche	*lecheh*	milk
manteca	*man-taker*	butter
mariscos	*mareeskos*	seafood
pan	*pan*	bread
papas	*papas*	potatoes
pescado	*peskado*	fish
pollo	*po-sho*	chicken
postre	*postreh*	dessert
potaje	*potaheh*	soup
sal	*sal*	salt
salsa	*salsa*	sauce
sopa	*sopa*	soup
té	*teh*	tea

Time

minute	**minuto**	*meenooto*
hour	**hora**	*ora*
half-hour	**media hora**	*med-ya ora*
Monday	**lunes**	*loones*
Tuesday	**martes**	*martes*
Wednesday	**miércoles**	*m-yairkoles*
Thursday	**jueves**	*hwebes*
Friday	**viernes**	*b-yairnes*
Saturday	**sábado**	*sabado*
Sunday	**domingo**	*domeengo*

Numbers

0	**cero**	*sairo*
1	**uno**	*oono*
2	**dos**	*dos*
3	**tres**	*tres*
4	**cuatro**	*kwatro*
5	**cinco**	*seenko*
6	**seis**	*says*
7	**siete**	*s-yeteh*
8	**ocho**	*ocho*
9	**nueve**	*nwebeh*
10	**diez**	*d-yes*
11	**once**	*onseh*
12	**doce**	*doseh*
13	**trece**	*treseh*
14	**catorce**	*katorseh*
15	**quince**	*keenseh*
16	**dieciséis**	*d-yeseesays*
17	**diecisiete**	*d-yesees-yeteh*
18	**dieciocho**	*d-yes-yocho*
19	**diecinueve**	*d-yeseenwebeh*
20	**veinte**	*baynteh*
30	**treinta**	*traynta*
40	**cuarenta**	*kwarenta*
50	**cincuenta**	*seenkwenta*
60	**sesenta**	*sesenta*
70	**setenta**	*setenta*
80	**ochenta**	*ochenta*
90	**noventa**	*nobenta*
100	**cien**	*s-yen*
500	**quinientos**	*keen-yentos*
1000	**mil**	*meel*

Selected Street Index

9 de Julio, Avenida	E2
25 de Mayo, Calle	F1
Acuña de Figueroa, Calle	K4
Adolfo Alsina, Calle	E2
Agote, Calle	N3
Agüero, Calle	L5
Agustín Pedro Justo, Plaza	G2
Alberti, Calle	C2
Alemania, Plaza	M2
Alicia Moreau de Justo, Avenida	G2
Almirante Brown, Avenida	G5
Alvear, Avenida	P4
Anchorena, Calle	M4
Andrés Berro, Avenida	M2
Antartida Argentina, Avenida	R5
Aráoz, Calle	K4
Arenales, Calle	N5
Argentina, Plaza	Q4
Aristóbulo del Valle, Calle	G5
Armenia, Calle	K3
Armenia, Plaza	K3
Austria, Calle	M4
Ayacucho, Calle	D1
Azcuénaga, Calle	C1
Azopardo, Calle	G3
Balcarce, Calle	F2
Bartolomé Mitre, Calle	D1
Belgrano, Avenida	F2
Bernardo de Irigoyen, Calle	E3
Billinghurst, Calle	M3
Bolívar, Calle	F2
Bonpland, Calle	J2
Boulogne Sur Mer, Calle	M5
Brandsen, Calle	G6
Brasil, Avenida	F4
Bulnes, Calle	M3
Cabello, Calle	M3
Cafferata, Calle	H6
Callao, Avenida	D1
Caminito, Calle	G6
Canada, Plaza	Q4
Carlos Calvo, Calle	E3
Carlos Pellegrini, Plazoleta	P4
Caseros, Avenida	D5
Castelli, Calle	C1
Castex, Calle	M2
Cavia, Calle	M2
Cecilia Gnerson, Boulevard	R5
Cerrito, Calle	E1
Cerviño, Avenida	K2
Chacabuco, Calle	F3
Charcas, Calle	M4
Chile, Calle	D3
Cochabamba, Calle	E4
Colombia, Avenida	L2
Combate de los Pozos, Calle	D2
Congreso, Plaza del	D2
Constitución, Calle	D4
Constitución, Plaza	E4
Copérnico, Calle	N3
Córdoba, Avenida	P5
Coronel Díaz, Avenida	M3
Correo, Plaza de	R6
Corrientes, Avenida	E1
Cortázar, Plaza (Plaza Serrano)	K3
Costa Rica, Calle	K3
D'Espósito, Calle	G4
Defensa, Calle	F2
Dorrego, Avenida	J2
Dorrego, Plaza	F3
Eduardo Madero, Avenida	G1
El Salvador, Calle	K4
Entre Ríos, Avenida	D2
Esmeralda, Calle	F1
Estado de Israel, Avenida	K5
Estados Unidos, Calle	F3
Florida, Calle	Q5
Fray Justo Santa María de Oro, Calle	K3
French, Calle	M4
Gallo, Calle	M4
Gascón, Calle	K4
General Juan D. Perón, Calle	D1
General L. Mansilla, Calle	L4
General Las Heras, Avenida	N3
General Lavalle, Plaza	P5
General Páez, Plaza	L2
Godoy Cruz, Calle	K3
Gorriti, Calle	K4
Grand Bourg, Plaza	N3
Guatemala, Calle	K3
Güemes, Calle	L3
Güemes, Plaza	L4
Guido, Calle	P4
Gurruchaga, Calle	K3
Gutierrez, Calle	L2
Haedo, Calle	P3
Hernandanas, Calle	F6
Hipolito Yrigoyen, Calle	D2
Honduras, Calle	K4
Humberto 1°, Calle	E3
Independencia, Avenida	F3
Infanta Isabel, Avenida	L1
Ing. Huergo, Avenida	G2
Intendente Bullrich, Avenida	K2
Intendente Seeber, Plaza	L2
Irala, Calle	F5
Iraola, Calle	L1
Islas Maldivas, Plaza	G4
Italia, Plaza	L2
Jean Jaures, Calle	M6
Jeronimo Salguero, Calle	L5
Jorge Luis Borges, Calle	K3
José Antonio Cabrera, Calle	K4
José E. Uriburu, Calle	C2
Juan B. Justo, Avenida	K2
Juan de Garay, Avenida	F4
Juan M. Blanes, Calle	G5
Juana Manso, Calle	G1
Jujuy, Avenida	B3
Julián Alvarez, Calle	L4
Julio A. Roca, Avenida	F2
Juncal, Calle	N4
Junín, Calle	C1
La Rábida, Avenida	G2
Lafinur, Calle	L2
Lamadrid, Calle	G6
Laprida, Calle	M4
Larrea, Calle	C1
Lavalle, Calle	Q6
Lavalleja, Calle	J5
Leandro N. Alem, Avenida	Q5
Lector, Plaza del	N3
Libertad, Calle	E1
Libertad, Plaza	P5
Libertador, Avenida del	N3
Lima, Calle	E2
Macacha Guemes, Boulevard	G1
Maipú, Calle	F1
Malabia, Calle	K3
Mansilla, Calle	M5
Manuela Gorriti, Calle	G2
Marcelo T. de Alvear, Calle	Q5
Mario Bravo, Calle	L5
Martín García, Avenida	F5
Martín Rodríguez, Calle	G6
Matheu, Calle	C2
Mayo, Avenida de	E2
Mayo, Plaza de	F1
Medicina, Plaza de	N5
Medrano, Avenida	K5
México, Calle	F2
Miserere, Plaza	B1
Misiones, Calle	C2
Montevideo, Calle	D1
Moreno, Calle	E2
Naciones Unidas, Plaza	N3
Nicaragua, Calle	K3
Olavarría, Calle	G6
Pacheco de Melo, Calle	N4
Pagano, Calle	N3
Palos, Calle	G5
Paraguay, Calle	Q5
Paraná, Calle	P5
Pasco, Calle	C2
Paseo Colón, Avenida	F2
Paso, Calle	C1
Pasteur, Calle	C1
Patricias Argentinas, Avenida	J6
Patricios, Avenida	F5
Pedro de Mendoza, Avenida	H6
Pellegrini, Calle	E1
Perú, Calle	F2
Pichincha, Calle	C2
Piedras, Calle	E3
Pinzón, Calle	G5
Posadas, Calle	P4
Presidente Figueroa Alcorta, Avenida	N3
Presidente Luis Sáenz Peña, Calle	D2
Presidente Quintana, Calle	P4
Presidente Ramón S. Castillo, Avenida	Q3
Pueyrredón, Avenida	N4
Reconquista, Calle	F1
República Árabe Siria, Calle	L2
República de Chile, Plaza	N3
República de la India, Calle	L2
República, Plaza de la	E1
Rincón, Calle	C2
Riobamba, Calle	N6
Rivadavia, Avenida	C1
Rodríguez Peña, Calle	D1
Rodríguez Peña, Plaza	N5
Roma, Plaza	R6
Roque Sáenz Peña, Avenida	E1
Rosales, Avenida	G1
Rosario Vera Peñaloza, Boulevard	G3
Russel, Calle	K3
Saavedra, Calle	C2
Salguero, Calle	N2
Salta, Calle	E2
San José, Calle	D2
San Juan, Avenida	E3
San Martín, Calle	Q6
San Martín de Tours, Calle	M2
San Martín, Plaza	Q5
Sanchez de Bustamante, Calle	M4
Santa Fe, Avenida	N5
Santa Rosa, Calle	K3
Santiago del Estero, Calle	E3
Sarandí, Calle	D1
Sarmiento, Avenida	L2
Sarmiento, Calle	Q6
Scalabrini Ortiz, Avenida	L3
Serrano, Calle	J4
Sicilia, Plaza	L2
Soler, Calle	L4
Solís, Calle	D2
Suárez, Calle	F6
Suipacha, Calle	E1
Tacuarí, Calle	E2
Talcahuano, Calle	E1
Thames, Calle	K3
Tucumán, Calle	Q6
Uriarte, Calle	K3
Uruguay, Calle	E1
Valentín Gómez, Calle	L6
Valle Iberlucea, Calle del	G6
Venezuela, Calle	F2
Viamonte, Calle	P5
Vicente López, Calle	N4
Vicente López, Plaza	P4
Virrey Cevallos, Calle	D2
Vittoria, Calle	N3